THE HESSIAN OCCUPATION OF NEWPORT AND RHODE ISLAND
1776–1779

OTHER BOOKS BY THE AUTHOR

Stars and Swastikas:
The Boy Who Wore Two Uniforms

Defenses of Narragansett
Bay in World War II

Dutch Island and Fort Greble

Davisville and the Seabees

Cover photo of Ansbach-Bayreuth diorama, *by Martin Goetz, Germany*

The Hessian Occupation of Newport and Rhode Island 1776-1779

Walter K. Schroder

HERITAGE BOOKS
2009

HERITAGE BOOKS
AN IMPRINT OF HERITAGE BOOKS, INC.

Books, CDs, and more—Worldwide

For our listing of thousands of titles see our website at
www.HeritageBooks.com

Published 2009 by
HERITAGE BOOKS, INC.
Publishing Division
100 Railroad Ave. #104
Westminster, Maryland 21157

Copyright © 2005 Walter K. Schroder

Other books by the author:
Stars and Swastikas: The Boy Who Wore Two Uniforms: Expanded Edition

All rights reserved. No part of this book may be reproduced or transmitted in any form or by any means, electronic or mechanical, including photocopying, recording or by any information storage and retrieval system without written permission from the author, except for the inclusion of brief quotations in a review.

International Standard Book Numbers
Paperbound: 978-0-7884-4074-8
Clothbound: 978-0-7884-8183-3

Dedicated

to all who fought and died

in the

Battle of Rhode Island

Contents

Foreword	XI
Preface	XV

Chapter 1   1
December 8, 1776: Occupation of Newport
Decision to Occupy Newport; Joint British-Hessian Expedition;
Landings and Deployments; Billeting Experiences;
The Chasseur Units; Early Tasking; General Prescott as Commandant

Chapter 2   9
Prelude to Hostilities
Background; Taxation; Defiance;
British Reactions; Evacuation of Boston

Chapter 3   19
Treaties for Troop Support
Britain Seeks Help; Commitment of Troops; Some Contractual Terms;
Hessians Outnumber All Others; The Franconians: Ansbach-Bayreuth;
Not All Hessians were Hessian; Mercenaries or Auxiliaries?

Chapter 4   27
The Troops
Hesse-Kassel Mobilization; Ansbach-Bayreuth Mobilization

Chapter 5   37
Troop Movements
The Overland Treks; Embarkation

Chapter 6   45
Crossing the Big Divide
First Division—Northern Atlantic Route; Sailed from Bremerlehe
to Portsmouth on April 17, 1776; Second Division—Southern
Atlantic Route, 1776; Sailed from Ritzebüttel to Portsmouth on
June 28, 1776; Voyage of the Ansbach-Bayreuth Regiments, 1777;
Other Impressions

Chapter 7   57
America
New York; Duty Calls

CHAPTER 8   63
NEWPORT
Social Matters and VIPs; Malsburg's Description of Newport;
The Fear of the Hessians; Seduction of Hessian Troops

CHAPTER 9   73
SOLDIERING IN SNOW AND ICE
The Close of 1776; Intentions Versus Reality

CHAPTER 10   79
1777—A TIME OF QUIET?
Troop Dispositions; Disappointments; Matters of Command;
Troop Reductions; The Prescott Kidnapping; Change-of-Command

CHAPTER 11   87
TROOP ADMINISTRATION
Staff Functions—The Quartermaster; The Auditor; The Surgeon;
The Chaplains; The Provost and the Advocate; Fraternization
and Marriage; Hessian Recordkeeping

CHAPTER 12   97
BRITISH DEFENSIVE MEASURES
Earlier Colonial Actions; Accession of Conanicut Island Resources;
British Accessions and Expansion in Newport; Disappointments
on Both Sides; Projects Go Forward

CHAPTER 13   107
RAIDS AND INCURSIONS
Off-Island Assignments and Happenings; Local Rotations;
The Bristol-Warren and Fall River Raids

CHAPTER 14   117
THE TREATY OF PARIS
All's Quiet in Newport; The Treaty of Paris; Maneuvers; More Troop
Movements; Anticipating the Arrival of French Fleet

CHAPTER 15   125
JUST IN TIME –THE 1778 TROOP REINFORCEMENTS
"Die Franken kommen!" Enemy Fleet on the Horizon

CHAPTER 16   135
THE 1778 SIEGE OF NEWPORT
A Time of Uncertainty; General Sullivan Moves on Newport;
French Fleet Departs; Siege Flounders

CHAPTER 17 THE BATTLE OF RHODE ISLAND Pigot Seizes Initiative; British Column Ambushed; The Battle Unfolds; What Next?	143
CHAPTER 18 AFTER THE BATTLE A Common Soldier's Assessment; Relief and Criticisms; Casualties; The Fall and Winter of 1778	153
CHAPTER 19 1779: TIME TO LEAVE Desperate Times; Duty as Usual; Plaudits; Honors; Complimenting the Enemy; Lost time; Losses	161
CHAPTER 20 CONCLUDING THOUGHTS Who Won?; Reminders; Return of the French; Final Words	171
BIBLIOGRAPHY	179
INDEX	189

FOREWORD

In *The Hessian Occupation of Newport and Rhode Island 1776–1779*, Walter Schroder has treated extensively with one of the major events of the American Revolution, which apart from some hard core groups of historical reenactors, has passed practically unknown into the mists of time. How many of the summer tourists headed for the fabled mansions of Newport pass unknowingly by some of the very houses that witnessed these historic events taking place at their very doorstep? Most native Rhode Islanders hurrying to their daily jobs in and around Newport, pass these sites, also unmindful of the historic events that occurred here over 225 years ago.

The Rhode Island campaign which lasted from 8 Dec 1776 to 25 Oct 1779 has unfortunately not been well recognized, even in Rhode Island. The reader should be deeply appreciative of the efforts of Mr. Schroder in so vividly bringing the events of this era to us in a very well researched and written historical narrative. His linguistic abilities and extensive use of original source diaries and unit journals, recorded in the German language, provide a wealth of hither to unavailable insights into the daily life of the German soldiers, committed to the Rhode Island campaign. Interestingly, there is a great deal of corroboration with the previous "gold standard," the diaries of British Lieutenant Frederick MacKenzie.

Mr. Schroder also brings a new perspective of the German allies of the British. In the victor's writing of history, the German soldier is usually portrayed as a mercenary and hireling. By referencing so much original German source material and describing the subsistence agreements, many of the myths relating to the status of these soldiers are laid to rest. He points out that such arrangements were not uncommon in 18th century Europe. In addition, we are also reminded of the still strong blood and family ties that existed between Britain's Hanoverian George III and the rulers of many of the German principalities, which facilitated such arrangements. Another fact correctly brought to our attention is that the individual German soldier, as with soldiers from time immemorial, is not the one who conducted affairs of state, but rather one who was duty bound to obey his sovereign, by the oath taken to support that sovereign. It is interesting to note that the German soldiers swore allegiance twice, first to their own prince, then at a later date, to the monarch of Great Britain. For those who see this as unusual, we can point to a similar modern practice, wherein the soldiers of the National Guard are first administered a Federal oath of office, and are then administered a State oath of office.

Today, when we can move thousands of soldiers and their equipment half way across the globe within forty-eight hours, we need to be reminded that it was far different in the 18th century. Mr. Schroder gives a close and personal look at the tremendous difficulties, dangers, and fears experienced by the common soldier as he moved across Europe to ports of embarkation for the perilous two month journey across the Atlantic to America. Use of original diaries and unit journals allows him to present the nearly three years of operations in Newport and around Aquidneck Island in a lively, detailed, and interesting manner that will be appreciated by all who read this work.

In his Concluding Thoughts, Mr. Schroder addresses the question, who won? This can perhaps be asked and answered on several different levels. Who won the campaign, and who won the Battle of Rhode Island that took place in August 1778? British arms obviously prevailed on both counts, as they always retained the ability to move their troops when and where they chose to do so, and were left in possession of the field on 29 Aug 1778. The Americans also most certainly won, when they were able to withdraw their army to the banks of the Sakonnet River, and in the face of the world's premier naval power, evacuate their troops across to the mainland.

However after reading this book and gaining a much deeper appreciation of the huge logistical and troop commitment to this campaign, one is tempted to develop another premise. That is to say, did the invasion and occupation of Newport squander limited Crown resources, especially as it degenerated into a "backwater" operation, to the extreme detriment of British arms and national policy? Consider the probable impact on the cause of American Freedom, had there been a reversal in the outcome of the Battle of Trenton on 26 Dec 1776, that was a must win for General Washington and the Continental Army. In the text, we are reminded that "Among the troops that had been put ashore in Newport on 8 Dec 1776 were some of the more seasoned Hessian Regiments that had played decisive roles in the victories at White Plains and New York." What if these troops had been posted to Trenton, rather than to the Newport invasion?

Again, what might have been the impact on the Battles of Saratoga, had all the troops been shifted to Quebec in the spring of 1777 to reinforce Burgoyne's army instead of protecting Newport, already an isolated outpost? Would Burgoyne's army invading New York from Canada have crushed the American defenders if they had another 10,000 troops? For Americans, achieving victory at Saratoga was again absolutely critical. Had they failed to gain that victory, the critical alliance with France may never have materialized, irrevocably dooming the cause of American Independence.

Through his extensive research, use of so many original German source documents, and obvious skills in organizing and writing, Mr. Schroder has contributed a work which expands greatly on our knowledge of the campaign in Rhode Island. Although this campaign is not usually viewed as being on a level with some of the better known and documented battles of the American Revolution, we are still left with a tantalizing question.

Was this major diversionary operation, so well detailed in this work, the key to critical American victories on not one, but two occasions, and ultimately to gaining independence from England?

BRIGADIER GENERAL RICHARD J. VALENTE, USA (RET)

Preface

My interest in the Hessian occupation of Newport and Rhode Island was first sparked in 1998, when I learned of plans to develop land adjacent to the Portsmouth Abbey, site of the August 29, 1778 Battle of Rhode Island. Though perhaps obscured by time, it was general knowledge that Hessian soldiers serving the King of England had fought against American colonists and suffered casualties on these grounds, just west of what today is known as West Main Road in Portsmouth, Rhode Island.

Who were these "Hessians"? Where did they come from? Were all Hessians truly Hessians? Were they mercenaries or auxiliary troops of the British? And, how and why did they ever do battle in Portsmouth, Rhode Island? These questions became the basis of my own curiosity. I soon discovered that published material on the Revolutionary War was indeed available, but also that very little, if anything, had been done in reporting the observations and experiences of these so-called Hessians. In particular there was little written on their three-year occupation of Rhode Island from 1776–1779, when they were a part of the British garrison in Newport.

Thus, I concentrated my research almost exclusively on the "Hessians," and in particular the several Regiments that took part in General Clinton's expedition and occupation of Rhode Island. In seeking credible information I referred to studies previously published in America and Germany, but also consulted with particular interest Hessian and Ansbach-Bayreuth diaries and journals, reading and often translating copies of preserved manuscripts that were made available to me by the repositories of the original historical records, here and abroad.

Past accounts of the British occupation of Newport and Rhode Island have drawn heavily on the Diary of Frederick MacKenzie, a British staff officer who served in Newport for the duration, concurrently recording in great detail the events of that time. Hessian officers, in particular Captain Friedrich von der Malsburg, their clergy, and even some of their enlisted men kept diaries and journals of their own. Taken together, many of these hand-written records now preserved in various archives add considerable detail to the information previously published, not only about the Hessians, but of the events in the Narragansett Bay area in general. The narrative which follows is a compilation of the stated data, intended to provide a more complete and rounded-out description of *The Hessian Occupation of Newport and Rhode Island, 1776–1779*.

The British-Hessian troop alignment during their northward advance from Newport on August 29, 1778, in pursuit of withdrawing American colonists resulted in the Hessians being assigned the area along West Main Road. Meanwhile the British proceeded northward by way of East Main Road, where they were ambushed by the rebels in a short but bloody engagement resulting in heavy losses. The Hessians, coming up on West Main Road, dislodged a rear-guard detail of colonists and soon after became embroiled in a protracted action in the fields adjacent to today's Portsmouth Abbey that lasted most of the day and became known as the Battle of Rhode Island.

In modern times, improvements of West Main Road in Portsmouth closed a short section of the older trail that ran across a marshy area through which the Hessians had advanced. One day, as I walked that isolated piece of country road, I observed a small overflowing creek with its damp and swampy surroundings and I could envision sweaty Hessian soldiers in their woolen uniforms making their way through and across this quagmire on that hot August day in 1778. From my research I knew they had lost some of their people during the battle who were buried nearby in what today is no more than a stretch of overgrown and soggy ground within a changed landscape. In their memory and honor I hummed the German tune *Auf Ansbach Dragoner, auf Ansbach-Bayreuth...* and I felt a presence... I knew their story should be told.

This record could not have been compiled without the coopera-

Preface

tion and help of many people with a scholarly knowledge of the described historical period, or with access to some of the lesser-known records and writings that ultimately became the backbone of my study.

First and foremost I wish to thank Horst Lochner, a dedicated friend and supporter from Bayreuth, Germany, for his untiring efforts in seeking out information on the Franconian troops deployed to Rhode Island. His enthusiasm was truly unmatched.

I respectfully acknowledge the cooperation of the Duke of Northumberland, England, an heir to Britain's Lord Percy, who commanded the Newport garrison in the early days of occupation, and of Gero von der Malsburg, Germany, a descendent of Captain Friedrich von der Malsburg, who so diligently recorded his observations of Newport, making his writings an integral part of Newport's Revolutionary War history heretofore not fully realized or appreciated.

The following individuals and their respective offices provided indispensible support in searching out and making available or acquiring critical research information so necessary to the successful outcome of this project. I greatly appreciate their support and responsiveness:

Dr. Inge Auerbach, Historian, University of Marburg, Germany

Dr. Arno Störkel, Historian, Würzburg, Germany

Dr. Marianne Heinz, Kassel State Museums, Germany

Peter Harrington, PhD, Curator,
 Anne S.K. Brown Military Collection, Brown University, RI

Robert A. Selig, PhD, Author-Historian

Andreas R. Bräunling, Stadtarchiv Dachau, Germany

Joan Youngken, Newport Historical Society, RI

Michael J. McAfee, Curator, U.S. Army West Point Museum, NY

Deborah Homer, Reference Librarian,
 Jamestown Philomenian Library, RI

Mr. Pimentel, Reference Librarian, Portsmouth Free Library, RI

Dr. Robert Behra, Reference Librarian, Redwood Library,
 Newport, RI

Brother Joseph, Portsmouth Abbey, RI

Earle N. Trickey, Middletown, RI

The following organizations supported my research in various ways for which I am deeply appreciative. Their cooperative responses to my needs became an inspiration to move the project along and through to completion:

Hessisches Staatsarchiv, Marburg, Germany
Historische Kommission für Hessen, Marburg, Germany
Historisches Museum, Stadt Bayreuth, Germany
Militärhistorisches Museum der Bundeswehr, Dresden, Germany
Staatsarchiv, Nürnberg, Germany
Verein für hessische Geschichte, Kassel, Germany
Rhode Island Committee for the Humanities
Rhode Island Historical Society Library, Providence
North Kingstown Free Library, RI
William Clements Library, University of Michigan, Ann Arbor, MI
Company of Military Historians, MA
Houghton Library, Harvard University, Cambridge, MA
The Huntington Library, San Marino, CA
The Library Company of Philadelphia, PA
Library of Congress, Washington, DC
The Mariners' Museum, Newport News, VA
The Miami Herald, Miami, FL
National Archives, Washington, DC
National Park Service, Washington, DC
The Johannes Schwalm Historical Association, NJ
U.S. Army Carlisle Barracks, PA

I extend a special word of thanks to Dr. Patrick T. Conley, Dr. John B. Hattendorf, and Dr. Albert T. Klyberg, for their valued comments and suggestions, and to Brigadier General Richard J. Valente, USA (Ret.), for offering the Foreword.

Last but not least, I wish to thank Martin Fox, my son-in-law, a scholar in his own right, for his interest and advice regarding the project, and for the many hours he devoted to editing my sometimes rough and challenging manuscript submittals. I also thank Jeffrey McDonough, publisher of *the Jamestown Press* and Jennifer Warren Benoit, for the outstanding job of shaping the manuscript into a well formatted and attractive piece of work.

I would be remiss if I would not acknowledge and thank my dear wife, Lora, for her patience and tolerance for the many times my mind strayed to matters of the past in pursuit of this project.

Walter K. Schroder
June 2005

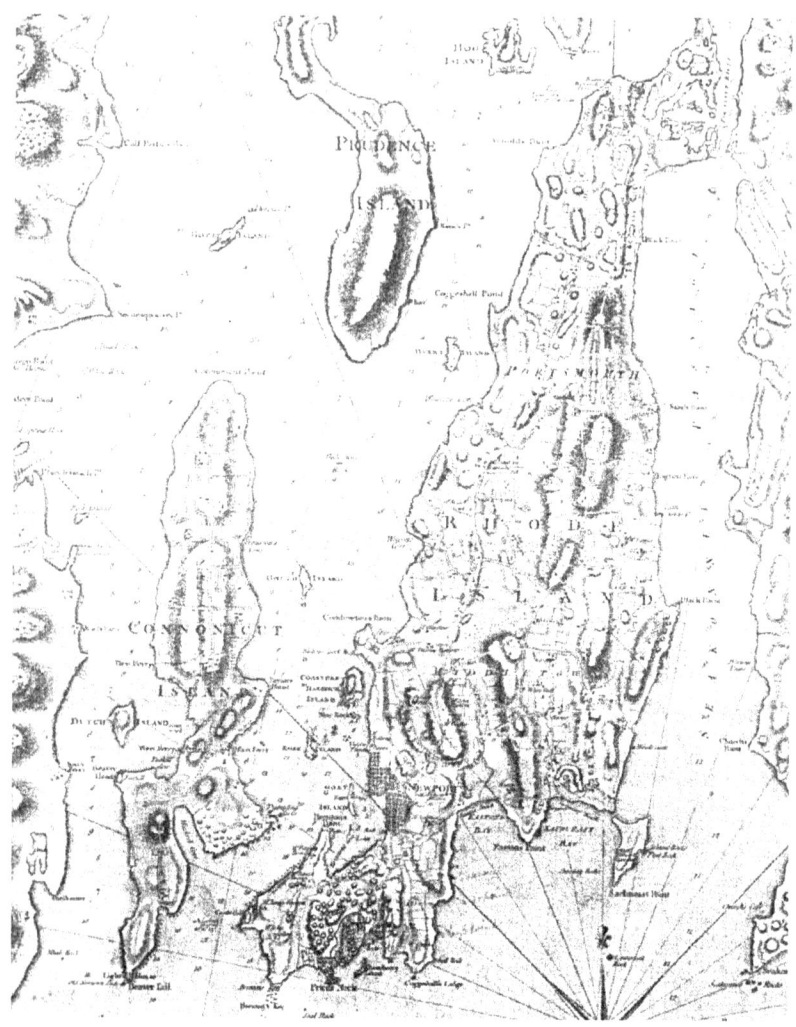

This section of the so-called *Blaskowitz Map*, presented to Hugh Earl Percy, Lieutenant General of His majesty's Forces in Great Britain and America, in 1777, encompases the areas in which the Hessians operated during the period 1776-1779. *University of Rhode Island Special Collections*

CHAPTER 1

December 8, 1776: Occupation of Newport

"One can hardly imagine how majestic the arriving fleet looked." These words, appearing in the *Journal of Regiment von Ditfurth* for December 7, 1776, as recorded by Hessian Quartermaster C. Wende, express the sentiments of some 6,500 British and Hessian troops who were standing by aboard a British armada of seven ships of the line plus four frigates and seventy transports, all poised and ready to enter Narragansett Bay and secure Newport.

DECISION TO OCCUPY NEWPORT

Earlier, in the fall of 1775, Britain's Lord Dartmouth suggested evacuating Boston and occupying Newport or New York with a significant military force. Newport, in his opinion, was the key to the control of the New England colonies. Boston was indeed evacuated by the British on March 17, 1776. Admiral Lord Richard Howe considered Newport the best site for a naval base in America. In addition, the area was appealing as a rest camp for troops after their long and sometimes arduous journey from Europe. His brother, General Sir William Howe, who was of the same opinion, ordered the detachment of about 6,500 men to effect the occupation of Newport and Rhode Island.

On November 20, Sir Henry Clinton began assembling the expeditionary force in New York, consisting of equal numbers of British and Hessian troops. The Hessians comprised the following six Regiments: Prinz Carl, DuCorps (Leib), von Ditfurth, Landgrave (Wutgenau), von Huyn, and von Bünau. The British contingent included four Regiments of Infantry, one of Artillery and a Corps of Light Horse. The Garrison Journal of the von Huyn Regiment notes that the troops marched to their embarkation points on November 25, with drums beating and flags flying.

The above Hessian units originally arrived in America during the period from August to October of 1776. One account of their earlier landings notes that many people fled their homes for fear of the Hessians, departing hastily and leaving their property behind as soon as they heard the deep sounds of the approaching drums. Prior to being tagged for the Rhode Island expedition, these troops had participated successfully in actions at Fort Washington and White Plains.

JOINT BRITISH-HESSIAN EXPEDITION

The British fleet sailed from New York on December 1, 1776, under Admiral Sir Peter Parker, Commander of British naval forces in Rhode Island. His destination: Newport and Narragansett Bay. The landing forces were under the command of Sir Henry Clinton and General Lord Hugh Percy, his second in command, under whom was Major General Richard Prescott, as well as Hessian Major General Martin Konrad Schmitt and Colonels F.W. von Lossberg and J.C. von Huyn.

The weather became stormy once the fleet entered open waters, resulting in many mishaps including broken masts, crashes, and injuries among the troops aboard ship. As the armada approached

The Attack on Rhode Island, December 8th, 1776 by Irwin Bevan.
The Bailey Collection, The Mariner's Museum, Newport News, Virginia

DECEMBER 8, 1776: OCCUPATION OF NEWPORT

Narragansett Bay on December 7, the weather and winds were more favorable for the anticipated landings.

Admiral Parker, in a precautionary move to protect his fleet against enemy fire that could be expected from cannon positioned along Newport's waterfront, chose to enter Narragansett Bay via the West Passage, utilizing the landmass of Conanicut Island as a shield for his ships. Even so, Lieutenant Frederick MacKenzie's diary records the sighting of a battery or redoubt with four embrasures facing the western channel that had been constructed by the rebels some two miles from the lighthouse, but appeared to have been abandoned. The fleet passed this site, more commonly known as Conanicut Battery, and sailed to the north end of the island without enemy interference, then maneuvered into position to ferry and land the troops on the western shore of Rhode Island, now referred to as Aquidneck Island. By late afternoon of December 7 the ships dropped anchor in the eastern channel near Dyer's Island opposite Weaver's Cove and about four miles from land.

Conanicut Battery earthworks, first spotted by Lt. Frederick MacKenzie as British fleet entered Narragansett Bay on December 8, 1776. *Author's photo*

LANDINGS AND DEPLOYMENTS

The landings got under way the following morning. Troops were shuttled in three waves to allow one-third of the men to be dropped off at Weaver's Cove and the empty boats to return to the transports at anchor in the channel for their next pick up. This process continued until all personnel had been landed, which was accomplished by mid-afternoon. Surprisingly, there was no resistance to the landing operation and it became clear that the enemy had effectively abandoned Newport. A few prisoners were brought in later in the day from among a group attempting to leave the north end of the island by ferry. The expeditionary forces were quick to move out and take possession of high ground and any abandoned entrenchments as far as the north end, some ten miles away. Concurrently, a British regiment put ashore in Newport and took possession of the town.

Hessian Landing by Jose Perez. *Courtesy Norah Pfeiffer*

Unable to bring their tents ashore due to heavy winds, many of the troops were forced to spend their first night in the open, exposed to severe winter weather. Their tents were brought ashore the following day and quickly set up. Those troops that had advanced toward more populated areas were able to find shelter in nearby homes and barns. For December 10, Lt. MacKenzie reported very hard frost, and ice an inch and a half thick. Even though arrangements were being made for most of the troops to move into winter quarters (i.e. shelters providing greater protection against the prevailing winter weather), it was necessary for several battalions of British and Hessian soldiers to remain encamped on the high ground just above the landing site for several additional days until they too could be assigned better housing. In the meantime they experienced an exceptionally heavy snowfall and high winds.

December 8, 1776: Occupation of Newport

Billeting Experiences

The Hessian Lossberg Brigade, consisting of the DuCorps, Prince Carl, and von Ditfurth Regiments moved into winter quarters in Newport, while the von Huyn Brigade—comprising the von Wutgenau, von Huyn and von Bünau Regiments—occupied houses, barns, and farms in various areas of the island to which they had been detailed.

Generally speaking, seven houses were assigned to each company in populated areas.

In some cases, soldiers were billeted with local civilian families. Where houses were taken, the barracks officer would furnish receipts to the town. These actions notwithstanding, many Newporters feared the Hessians based on negative reports that preceded their arrival and avoided contact with them during the early days of the occupation. The following excerpts taken from the diary of Capt. Friedrich von der Malsburg of the von Ditfurth Regiment, reflect the mood of the time as seen through the eyes of this officer:

Friday, December 13, 1776

> ...assigned to house owned by Elay Sheffield, opposite Coaster Harbor Island. People feel the military presence is disrupting their normal lives. Thanks to a kind old woman, I found a very nice room furnished with mahogany furniture. Elay Sheffield is one of the more fortunate inhabitants of this island who made his money on the sea trade offered here. Nearby on Tonomy Hill I came upon an uncompleted fort that would have served well against a land attack on the city. From here, the city is one mile away.

Saturday, December 14

> ... Had to leave my new billets on orders for the regiment to move to winter quarters in Newport... We assembled outside the city and at 2:00 p.m. marched in with resounding music. We put up in houses where the inhabitants, perhaps being rebels, had left or feared us enough to leave. Our regiment was assigned to 12–14 such vacant houses. All that was there were the bare walls. An old matron who had stayed behind went around to her neighbors and provided several chairs and tables

for my use. If I had my choice I would have stayed in the quarters I was required to vacate today. Evening music in the company of General Clinton and Lord Percy.

About the same time, a Hessian contingent went into winter cantonment on the east side of the island while several members of Colonel von Huyn's staff took up residence at Whitehall (also known as the Berkeley house). Although Hessian troops wore woolen uniforms, their clothing was no match for the extremely harsh winter climate they were experiencing in the Newport area. It was not until January 1777 that they were supplied with much-needed woolen jackets, gloves, and shoes.

"Whitehall" in Middletown was requisitioned by the staff of Colonel von Huyn. *Author's photo*

THE CHASSEUR UNITS

Blanket material was made available to each of the men who had been hand-picked to serve in two specially organized Chasseur units so they could make leggings to wear with their uniforms. Chasseurs were much like the British Light Infantry or Hessian Jäger units who were trained for rapid maneuvering and often served as avant guards. Since the expeditionary force did not include a Jäger unit, two Chasseur companies were formed from members drawn from the Landgrave, von Ditfurth, von Huyn, and von Bünau Regiments. Captain Friedrich von der Malsburg of the von Ditfurth Regiment commanded the 1st Company, and Captain August Christian Noltinius of the von Bünau Regiment, the 2nd Company. Combined, the two companies numbered 154 personnel, including four drummers. The men wore the uniforms of their original regiments and were armed with a musket, bayonet, and sabre. The officers and non-commissioned officers carried short muskets. Because of their around-the-clock alert status and constant readiness for special assignments they were exempt from normal garrison duties.

While taking possession of and assessing abandoned rebel entrenchments and cannon in the Newport area, the British 54th Regiment moved a force of 100 men to Conanicut Island on December 12 to bring it under the control of the Crown. The remainder of the Regiment followed on December 20. Basic earthworks thrown up at Butts Hill by the Americans (referred to as Windmill Hill by the Hessians and British) at the north end of Rhode Island were taken over and strengthened. Additional works were added at Quaker, Turkey, and Anthony Hills. Lawton's Valley and the Glen were also earmarked for the construction of defensive works. The existing earthworks on Miantonomi Hill (called Tonomy Hill by the Hessians) were expanded, making them into the citadel of the town.

EARLY TASKING

Later in December, a 200-man task force sailed to Long Island aboard six transports to cut and fetch wood for the Newport garrison. This was necessitated by the extreme winter weather conditions, combined with a critical shortage of firewood on Rhode Island. About that time, Lieutenant MacKenzie noted in his diary that a bottle of water standing under his bed had frozen solid as did a bottle of ink he had kept inside a desk in his room.

GENERAL RICHARD PRESCOTT AS COMMANDANT

On December 18, Major General Prescott was made Commandant of the City of Newport, with Lieutenant Colonel Campbell being named his Deputy. It is said that Prescott never hesitated to use his cane on citizens who were tardy in saluting him, and that he commandeered for his own comfort anything that suited his fancy. Life under General Prescott is alleged to have been unbearable; punishments were severe, some resulting in desertions and suicides. He arranged to be quartered at the home of Mr. Overing on West Main Road, near the Portsmouth-Middletown line, some five miles outside the center of Newport.

German-speaking Troops Assigned to Newport

Troops of Landgrave Friedrich II of Hessen
From Hessen - Kassel Area

Dec 7, 1776 – May 18, 1777
DuCORPS - LEIB Regiment
PRINZ CARL, Musketeer Regt

Dec 7, 1776 – Oct 25, 1779
von DITFURTH, Fusilier Regt
von BÜNAU, Garrison Regt
von HÜYN, Garrison Regt
LANDGRAF (Wutgenau)

Troops of Margrave Friedrich
Carl Alexander From: Ansbach-Bayreuth
Jul 16, 1778 – Oct 25, 1779
ANSBACH Regt (von Voit)
BAYREUTH Regt (von Seybothen)

CHAPTER 2

Prelude to Hostilities

Background

The troubles Britain faced in maintaining control over its colonial possessions in North America, which culminated in the American Revolution of 1776–1783, can be traced in part to the debts resulting from Britain's earlier involvement in the Seven Years' War of 1756–1763, or the French and Indian War, as it was known in America.

Much of Europe had been drawn into this prolonged conflict in which France, Austria, Saxony, Sweden, and Russia were pitted against Great Britain, Hanover, and Prussia. While this developed into a history-making land war for the Prussians under Frederick II (Frederick the Great), France and England were sparring over the control of North America and India. The latter confrontation began in 1754 and ended in the Treaty of Paris on February 10, 1763, with Britain emerging as the dominant colonial power. At that time, it had discontinued financial support of Prussia. Nevertheless, that phase of the war concluded in Prussia's favor soon after.

The Treaty of Paris brought with it additional responsibilities for Britain, namely the allocation of troops to secure the territories it acquired from France and Spain while at the same time providing protection of the Indians in those areas. The national debt and taxes were the most pressing issues facing Britain during the immediate postwar period. It has been estimated that these debts amounted to from 114 to 133 million pounds sterling. Thus, only a mere 6,000 soldiers could be allocated to the area of North America to accomplish all of the required tasks. This necessitated the establishment of military strong points in New York and Pennsylvania.

Newport was a major colonial city, along with Boston, New York, Philadelphia, and Charleston. The slave trade was blossoming in Newport, Bristol, and Providence. It has been estimated that half of all Newporters were in some way connected with the slave trade as early as 1760, and that a higher percentage of slaves were being kept than in any other northern colony, many at large plantations in Narragansett. Of the 184 ships in the colony, many were engaged in the slave business, trading rum for negroes in Africa.

Britain's Navigation Acts required strict regulation of colonial trade. This regulation included the stationing of British ships of war at the entrance to Narragansett Bay for the purpose of searching and seizing any ships in violation of the acts of trade. Similar actions were taken at the other colonies.

TAXATION

To raise urgently needed revenues to absolve Britain's wartime debts, the British Cabinet developed measures during the latter part of 1763 to provide for better control of the colonies and to raise taxes from within. In 1764 new taxes like the Sugar Act were levied on the colonists about which they had no input or control. The Stamp Act of 1765 required revenue and tax stamps to be affixed or imprinted upon any legal and trade documents as well as publications, for which the colonists were expected to pay. Selling of non-stamped newspapers, printed matter, playing cards, and dice games were punishable. In addition, documents without the required stamps were not accepted by the courts as evidence. The Sugar Act also hit home very hard in Newport since it restricted importation of sugar and molasses for its distilleries, which were a vital link in their overseas trading ventures. These and related actions by their Sovereign resulted in discontent and protestations on behalf of those affected.

As a counter-action, merchants in the colonies began to boycott British goods. Although the Stamp Act was rescinded, it did not take long for Charles Townshend to call for greater taxes to make up for certain property tax relaxations granted large land owners in England. Enforcement of duties in the colonies became vital, thus a customs agency was established in Boston and protected by two English regiments that were sent there for that purpose. When the Parliament of New York refused to provide support to British troops that were stationed there, it was promptly suspended.

Prelude to Hostilities

Defiance

By 1769 the patience of the discontented colonists was coming to an end. In Newport there was open defiance in July of that year when the British sloop *Liberty* (previously confiscated from John Hancock) was torched and scuttled. On March 5, 1770 there was open insurrection in Boston against the Townshend Laws. The British 29th Regiment confronted the protesters on King Street and opened fire, killing five civilians. This act became known as the "Boston Massacre."

The bloody massacre perpetuated in King Street, Boston, on March 5, 1770. Engraving by Paul Revere, 1770. *Courtesy Glen Cockrum*

Perhaps the first major act of the American Revolution was the burning of the British ship *Gaspee* at Namquit Point, Warwick, by a band of patriots on June 10, 1772 at which time the captain of the *Gaspee* was shot and wounded. Tensions grew in Newport and the Sons of Liberty were openly protesting the Townshend Trade Act.

The British ships *St. John*, the *Maidenstone*, and the *Squirrel* were also subjected to rebel attacks.

The East India Company was having financial problems, but received assistance from the British. The Bostonians in turn protested the importation of taxed tea and the stationing of troops in their town. Tempers built up until, on December 16, 1773, three loads of tea were thrown into Massachusetts Bay by colonists clad as Indians in what is recorded as the "Boston Tea Party." From that day forward both the British and the colonists were preparing for open confrontation. By the end of the following year, a total of eleven Royal Regiments were stationed in the Boston area, as both sides hardened their stands. In the meantime the so-called Quartering Act, an edict to billet troops in private homes had been imposed on the colonists. This demand only hardened their negative attitudes. All in all, the British actions implemented from 1763 to 1774 brought about increased distrust and controversy between the parties. Meanwhile, in November 1774, Captain James Wallace, commanding *H.M.S. Rose* began monitoring traffic on Narragansett Bay, stopping and searching many ships, thereby creating an even greater dislike of the British Crown's enforcers.

The destruction of tea at Boston Harbor. Lithograph by Sarony and Major, 1846. *Courtesy Glen Cockrum*

H.M.S. Rose, under command of Captain James Wallace, patrolled the waters of Narragansett Bay in the years prior to the major troop landings of December 1776. *The Miami Herald*

By then the Continental Congress was considering taking countermeasures, first suggesting a meeting with their British counterparts. The idea of such a meeting was dismissed in England as being without legal foundation.

Open warfare began on April 19, 1775 when British General Gage marched to Concord with 700 men to destroy a cache of the militia's ammunition stored there. His plans became known, resulting in a skirmish with the locals at Lexington. Soon after suffering their first casualties, the colonists—or rebels as the British branded them—took up arms and engaged in a full-fledged armed confrontation that lasted but a short time. By day's end, however, the British had suffered 300 casualties and the Militia seventy. This engagement had far-reaching consequences, as it represented the first armed resistance against the British Crown and signaled the beginning of open conflict.

That same day a force of 1,000 men from Providence was dispatched to Lexington to assist their embattled brethren.

On June 15, the Continental sloop *Katy* overcame the British sloop *Diana*, a tender of the *H.M.S. Rose*, stationed in Narragansett Bay. Soon after, a Continental Navy was formally established.

BRITISH REACTIONS

The rapidly deteriorating situation in North America prompted Lord Dartmouth in the Fall of 1775 to recommend the British evacuation of Boston and the occupation of Newport or New York by strong military forces. He felt a determined presence in Newport would be needed as a basis for controlling the other colonies in New England.

About that time, on August 23, 1775, King George III issued a proclamation calling for suppression of the insurgency, which made the colonists more determined to fight a War for Independence.

Captain Wallace fell in line with the Crown's edict by raiding Conanicut Island on December 10, 1775, with a force of 200 British troops. The uniformed detail under his command landed at East Ferry and marched across the island where the ferry house and as many as thirteen other buildings were torched, while some fifty cows, oxen, and a number of sheep and hogs were rounded up and

PRELUDE TO HOSTILITIES 15

Reenactors demonstrate the burning of houses by British troops.
Courtesy Earle N. Trickey

taken away by the raiding party. A resulting exodus of island residents decreased the population from 556 in 1775 to 323 in 1776. Prudence Island did not escape the wrath of Captain Wallace, who raided that small island repeatedly.

At that time Britain's Army consisted of 48,000 men, of which 8,500 were in America.

Given the recent unfavorable developments, there existed a definite need for reinforcements to maintain necessary controls in the colonies. The British situation was difficult to manage considering the distances between the garrisons in America and the top decision makers in England. This difficulty was compounded by the time it took to contact the Motherland and receive any necessary replies, as all such communications were transported and delivered by ship.

Britain initially solicited the assistance of Empress Catherine the Great of Russia in search for an established and experienced military force that could be quickly thrown into the breach to restore law and order in North America. Although troops were readily available at the time, the request was not met in part due to pressures exerted by Frederick the Great of Prussia.

Based on earlier offers received from German princes that had

16 THE HESSIAN OCCUPATION

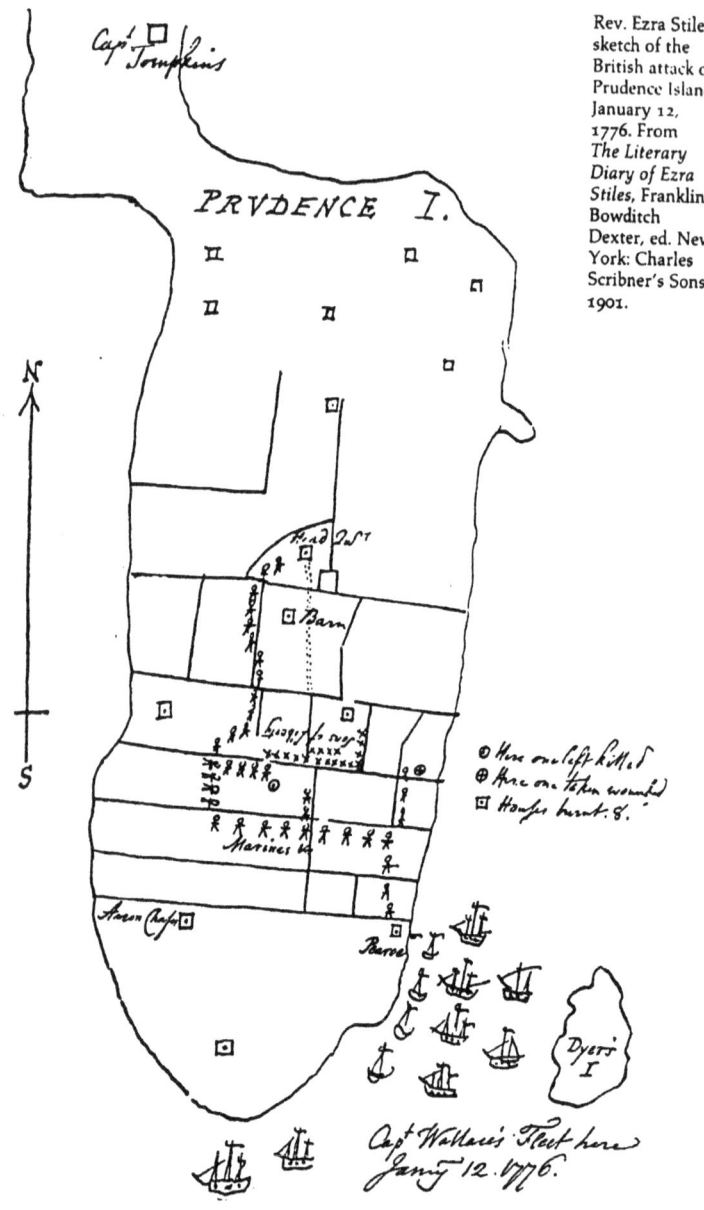

Rev. Ezra Stiles' sketch of the British attack on Prudence Island, January 12, 1776. From *The Literary Diary of Ezra Stiles*, Franklin Bowditch Dexter, ed. New York: Charles Scribner's Sons, 1901.

Sketch of the British raid on Prudence Island, January 12, 1776.

PRELUDE TO HOSTILITIES 17

not been accepted, Lord Suffolk, Britain's Minister of State, dispatched Colonel William Faucitt to Germany late in 1775, to persuade the princes to furnish the required troops in return for revenues that could help alleviate some of their own financial troubles. In addition to the territories of the King of Prussia in the north and certain hereditary Austrian dominions in the south, Germany at the time was made up of many small states and principalities consisting of several hundred sovereignties owned or controlled by princes, landgraves, margraves and bishops, a number of free cities, and in excess of some 1,000 estates of Imperial Knights. Each of these political entities was required to maintain its own petty prince and court, and based on the circumstances of the times, an army sufficient to protect its interests, never knowing who might have designs to annex or absorb a smaller neighbor's territory.

Colonel Faucitt arrived in Germany by the end of 1775 to establish contact with and seek support from among the German Princes who had previously been aligned with Britain in the Seven Years' War of 1756–1763.

While on this mission, the situation in North America was continuing to deteriorate. In January 1776, Brigadier General Esek Hopkins of the Newport Company of Militia was ordered to prepare defensive positions at Beavertail on Conanicut Island, sufficient to accept six to eight cannon. During that same time period, Captain Wallace was continuing his raids of isolated sites in the Narragansett Bay area. On January 12 he put a force of 250 men ashore on Prudence Island, this time burning seven dwellings and rounding up some sheep. Fighting ensued when colonists arrived from Warren and Bristol and confronted his party. Soon afterward the British withdrew or were driven off, leaving several of their dead behind.

EVACUATION OF BOSTON

When Lord Howe evacuated Boston on March 17, 1776, Boston had effectively been lost due to the armed rebellion of the colonists. Valuable equipment was left behind as the British departed and sailed for Halifax, where they remained until advised that reinforcements were en route from Europe. They then sailed for New York to meet up with the newly arriving troops. Meanwhile, on May 4, Rhode Island renounced its allegiance to Great Britain's

King George III, an event followed two months later by the adoption of the Declaration of Independence on July 4, 1776.

CHAPTER 3

Treaties for Troop Support

BRITAIN SEEKS HELP

Empowered by Britain's King George III, Colonel William Faucitt visited the Princes of Brunswick and Hesse-Kassel to seek their support in making troops available for deployment to the North American continent. He first contacted the Duke of Brunswick-Wolfenbüttel, a brother-in-law to the King, and was able to conclude a so-called "Subsidy Agreement" with Brunswick on January 9, 1776 for the provision of 5,723 troops. He signed a similar treaty with the Landgrave of Hesse-Kassel on January 15, 1776, for 12,500 of his soldiers. This became the sixth time in one hundred years that Hesse-Kassel had hired out its troops under treaty. As with Brunswick, there also existed a relationship through marriage between Landgrave Friedrich II of Hesse-Kassel and the King, in that the Landgrave's first wife had been the daughter of British King George II. The support of both Princes had been solicited by Britain. George III was King of Great Britian and Ireland, and elector (and later King) of Hanover. He was the son of Frederick Louis, price of Wales, and Princess Augusta of Saxe-Gotha. A member of the House of Hanover, he was the first to be born and educated as an Englishman. Aware of the King's urgent need for troops and the financial rewards that would result from providing required manpower, the Princes of Hesse-Hanau, Waldeck, and somewhat later, Anhalt-Zerbst and Ansbach-Bayreuth also offered their services and assistance to the King.

COMMITMENT OF TROOPS

The use of subsidy agreements to secure the services of foreign troops for one's own purposes when needed was a beneficial alter-

William Woolett's print of King George III.
Clements Library, University of Michigan [Ann Arbor, MI]

native to maintaining large standing armies. Even large and powerful countries could not afford the luxury of maintaining military forces in excess of reasonable needs for long periods of time. Because of their own serious financial shortcomings, German princes were very much inclined to enter into these contractual arrangements with Britain so they might benefit from the financial returns that would result from selling the services of their troops. There already existed historic precedents for Germans serving away from home and under foreign flags in return for pay. In 1776 the subsidy agreements were consummated between German princes and the British crown. While there existed laws that prevented selling the services of individual citizens to a foreign country, entire military units were permitted to serve as what amounted to allies, for a period of time regulated by treaty. The anticipated financial gains were regarded by the Princes as acceptable means of overcoming poverty among their people while at the same time making it possible to improve public facilities, raise standards of living, and make improvements to their own castles, as well as other cultural assets within the principality, such as art galleries, universities, libraries and opera houses.

Empowerment Documentation and Signatures on the Subsidy Agreement of 1777 between Britain and Ansbach-Bayreuth.
Stadtarchiv Nürnberg, Germany

SOME CONTRACTUAL TERMS

While most of the treaties had provisions that were common to all, not all agreements were neccessarily identical with each other. It was most common that the Principality agreed to furnish and maintain legal control as well as discipline over an agreed-upon number of well-trained and equipped troops along with their own officers, and supply their troops with necessary equipment. The furnishing of replacement personnel for any casualties suffered was the responsibility of the prince. Initially, the princes would receive a fee of 50 Thalers per man covered under the agreement. In addition, they were entitled to an annual subsidy payment of 125 Thalers per soldier. Although the men had sworn allegiance to their own sovereigns, they were required to give a second oath of allegiance to the King of Britain before embarking on their journeys across the Atlantic. In

Landgrave Friedrich II of Hesse by Tischbein, 1875.
Staatliche Museen Kassel, Germany

addition to certain common language, the subsidy treaties with Brunswick, Waldeck, and Hanau contained so-called "blood money" provisions, obliging the King to make specially agreed-upon payments for all men killed in action or taken prisoner and not returned. Britain did pay for casualties attributed to death and wounds, but not for the loss of personnel due to desertion.

Hessians Outnumber All Others

By far the largest contingent of troops was furnished by Landgrave Friedrich II of Hesse-Kassel, estimated at some 12,500 personnel. By the end of the American Revolutionary War he had made available close to 17,000 men. His initial contribution to the King's cause consisted of fifteen infantry regiments of five companies each, four grenadier battalions, one Jäger corps, and two batteries of artillery. The grenadier battalions were newly formed for service in America. All other troops supplied by Hesse-Kassel were from the Landgrave's regular army, a 16,000-man strong force trained and disciplined under Prussian rules.

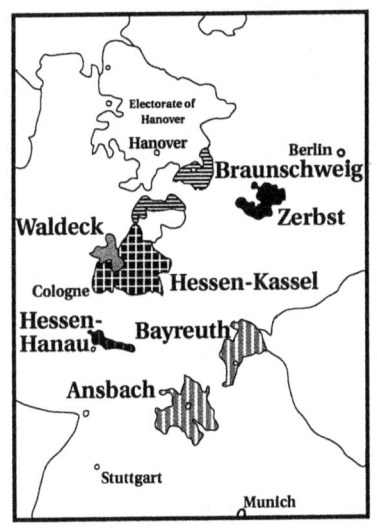

Subsidy Contracts
Troops solicited by King George III

- Jan 9, 1776 Braunschweig (Brunswick) 5,723
- Jan 15, 1776 Hessen-Kassel (Hesse-Cassel) 17,000

Troops offered to King George III

- Feb 6, 1776 Hessen-Kassel (Hesse-Hanau) 2,600
- Apr 20, 1776 Waldeck 1,226
- Feb 1, 1777 Ansbach-Bayreuth 3,393
- Oct 1777 Anhalt-Zerbst 1,119 (5% of population)

Brunswick supplied 5,723 troops while Hesse-Hanau provided 2,600 and Waldeck 1,226. Anhalt-Zerbst produced 1,119 soldiers, representing 5% of the principality's population. Overall, Hesse-Kassel contributed more than half of all auxiliary troops deployed to North America in support of Britain's efforts to put down the

Margrave Carl Alexander of Brandenburg Ansbach-Bayreuth.
Historisches Museum Bayreuth, Germany

rebellion and reestablish British control over its American colonies. The agreements with Anhalt-Zerbst and Ansbach-Bayreuth were formalized in 1777 – i.e. after the 1776 round of treaties had been executed and the troops shipped to America.

THE FRANCONIANS: ANSBACH-BAYREUTH

Margrave Christian Friedrich Carl Alexander of Ansbach-Bayreuth consummated a subsidy contract with Britain on February 1, 1777. Under this agreement Ansbach-Bayreuth would make available to the King two single battalion regiments of infantry, a company of Jägers, and one company of artillery initially—a total of 1,140 personnel. Subsequently, larger groups of reinforcements were provided, boosting the number to a total of 2,353. Originally, Ansbach and Bayreuth had been separate entities, each with its own

Margrave. When the last Margrave of Bayreuth died in 1765, Carl Alexander of Ansbach inherited his holdings as the rightful heir, thus becoming Margrave of Ansbach-Bayreuth. His mother had been a sister of Frederick the Great of Prussia. Burdened by the heavy debts he had inherited, Margrave Carl Alexander offered his troops to Britain as early as 1775, and again in 1776, but was turned down each time. It was not until February of 1777 that Britain reconsidered his offer and consummated the subsidy contract with Ansbach-Bayreuth. This became the first time Ansbach or Bayreuth had entered into such a treaty, after declining an earlier arrangement with Holland in 1743.

NOT ALL HESSIANS WERE HESSIAN

Since the largest number of the earlier recruited soldiers had originated from Hesse-Kassel, it became common practice of the British as well as the Americans to refer to all German subsidy troops as Hessians. This is incorrect. Soldiers from other principalities such as Waldeck, Anhalt-Zerbst, Brunswick, and Ansbach-Bayreuth were by no means Hessians, nor did they wish to be referred to as such. The only other bonafide Hessians that had been recruited hailed from Hesse-Hanau.

MERCENARIES OR AUXILIARIES?

Throughout much of American literature the German subsidiary or auxiliary troops are described as "mercenaries," giving the false impression they were soldiers of fortune, or perhaps even foreign legionnaires; i.e. undisciplined and irresponsible second-rate individuals who would sell their bodies and military skills for a good price, and who were willing to serve under foreign flags and officers, prepared to carry out any mission to which they might be assigned. Branding the Hessian troops as "mercenaries" may have resulted from misunderstanding the facts surrounding their recruitment and service, and may also be traced in part to negative American propaganda during the War of Independence aimed at discrediting the enemy, combined with the attitudes of later writers recording history from the point of view of the victor without giving much credence to the other side. While the use of the designation "mercenary" may have been degrading to the Hessians, psychologically it may have helped boost the morale of the local populace, thereby bolstering their willingness to fight against their British antagonists.

Some of the points that may have been missed or disregarded by those identifying the Hessian auxiliary troops as "mercenaries" are worth considering as part of any serious assessment of that term. First and foremost, it must be realized that it was the Landgrave who had signed the contract obligating personnel of his army to serve the King of England, for which he personally received the benefit of that obligation in the form of sizeable periodic subsidy payments. The individual soldier did not fight for monetary gain, nor did he have any choice as to whom he would fight for or against. Generally speaking, a soldier's pay amounted to approximately three pounds and ten pence per year. This cannot be considered the pay of a mercenary. By way of a second oath of allegiance, the soldier became a servant of the King and remained loyal to him, while at the same time maintaining his allegiance to his own Landgrave under the arrangement of double allegiances. Another important point worthy of note is that the Landgrave retained the right to withdraw his troops from America in case of an emergency necessitating their services in their homeland. The foregoing points have been stressed as being supportive of more appropriate alternative designations for these Hessian troops, such as auxiliaries or perhaps even allies.

Politically, an alignment by treaty with King George III provided needed security and assurances to the participating princes that Britain would come to their aid in the event a situation arose at home that might threaten these sovereigns, for which military support could become essential.

CHAPTER 4

Mobilization and Recruitment

Soon after ratification of the first four subsidy agreements, (i.e. those consummated in early 1776), the princes initiated necessary mobilization and recruitment actions to ready the troops they had committed to serving the King's objectives in America. The troops from Brunswick and Hesse-Hanau were dispatched to Quebec, arriving on June 1, 1776, followed by a second contingent that arrived in July, with some landing by the end of September, 1776. These particular troops participated in battles at Ticonderoga, Bennington, Saratoga, Freeman's Farm, Bemis Heights, and others.

Following the departure of the Brunswickers and Hesse-Hanauers, Hesse-Kassel and Waldeck were preparing to send their troops to staging areas in New York.

Hesse-Kassel Mobilization

Although Landgrave Friedrich II of Hesse-Kassel had always maintained an exceptionally well-trained and well-equipped army, it became necessary to bring any understaffed units up to strength quickly. This was accomplished by recalling all furloughed personnel and initiating recruitment actions to fill any vacancies that existed in the ranks. This recruitment was essential in order to staff and equip four new grenadier battalions that were to be especially formed for service in America.

Ever since 1762, there existed in Hesse-Kassel regulations prescribing acceptable behavior and procedures as well as prohibitions governing the recruitment process. The recruiting aim was to enlist only those who could be spared, since most of the able-bod-

Landgrave Friedrich II of Hesse-Kassel inspecting the Guard about 1770.
Staatliche Kunstsammlung Kassel, Germany

ied men came from families of farmers.

Following the signing of the subsidy contracts, a special push was initiated to seek out so-called foreigners for enlistment, i.e. anyone from outside one's own principality. This should not be construed as meaning foreigners from outside the broader German area. Likewise, it was forbidden to use force in the enlistment process, although this rule was not strictly adhered to with the foreigners. The regulations further pointed out that those needed to work the farms and trades were to be exempted from military service, but that anyone faking an illness that could not be verified by physical examination would be drafted first. Generally, the minimum height of any recruit was set at no less than 5'6" and the age between 16 and 30 years. Since these procedures represented a form of "Required Military Service," it can be appreciated that lists of eligibles were maintained and musters held periodically to track the whereabouts and availability of potential recruits within the principality. The rules were publicized by ringing church bells and reading the proclamations.

In order to make recruiting more equitable, the Landgrave of Hesse-Kassel issued a written order effective October 1, 1774,

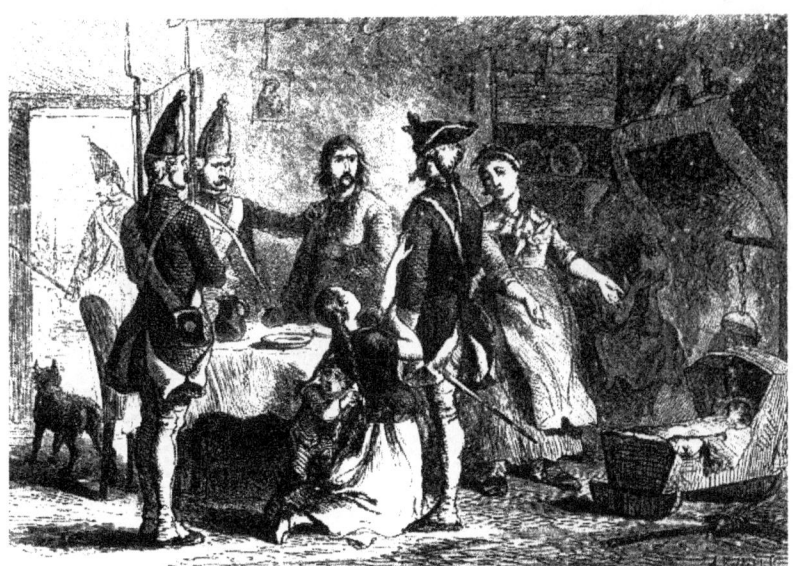
Darley's drawing of German soldiers being drafted for service in America.
Courtesy Dover Publications

under which each of his regiments was assigned a specific geographical area and certain named settlements from where they were permitted to draw or solicit their required numbers of recruits. These procedures aimed to insure that recruiting would be spread more evenly among the population, preventing more aggressive recruiters from picking and choosing the best candidates from any locale of their choice. The instruction went beyond the stated division of areas and towns by breaking these down even further and assigning subordinate recruiting areas to individual companies within the regiments.

The city of Marburg was exempt from recruitment; however, commencing in 1777, when new recruits were being sought, the city used this opportunity to get rid of some of their less desirable citizens. It is said that some women tried to rid themselves of their abusive husbands by this means. On the other hand there were also women, in fact families, who traveled overseas with their soldiers.

Hesse-Kassel had an army numbering some 16,000 personnel that had been trained, drilled, and equipped in the way of the Prussians. They were well-disciplined and for the most part their officers were career soldiers with good educations. Landgrave

Recruiting Guidlines issued by Landgrave Friedrich II of Hesse-Kassel in 1774. *University of Marburg, Germany*

Friedrich II enjoyed drilling his troops personally. It is said that for lack of a drill hall he exercised up to 300 men in the dining hall of his castle during inclement weather. In anticipation of serving in North America, troops were drilled in deep snow to prepare them for the harsh climate they would be expected to encounter.

As might be expected, most of the petty princes prescribed Potsdam or Prussian blue uniforms for their troops. This was perhaps a sign of identifying with Prussia, the nearest land-based super power, and a gesture to their hoped-for protector if ever they were in desperate need of military assistance. This hope was held despite the fact that Frederick the Great of Prussia looked with displeasure upon the idea of contracting out troops to Britain. He felt such deals could only be motivated by the greed of the petty princes. Besides, he expressed his feelings that the war in America ought not to be of any concern to them.

The 12,500 Hesse-Kassel troops initially designated to make the trip across the Atlantic consisted primarily of fusilier, musketeer,

Mobilization and Recruitment

grenadier, Jäger, and garrison units as well as necessary artillery support. The designation of these units refers generally to their function or specialty. Fusiliers were armed with a fusel, or light flintlock musket; musketeers were armed with a musket; while grenadiers were foot soldiers trained to throw grenades, i.e. small round bombs of the type in use for almost 100 years at that time. These were tall and specially trained men. Along with the grenadiers, the Jägers/chasseurs were recognized as the elite troops of Hesse-Kassel. The latter received their designation from the German word for hunters because of their ability to stalk their prey and their flexibility to move quickly in any type of terrain, having derived the basis of their special skills from earlier outdoor work or as woodsmen. The Jägers could be distinguished from all other Hessian troops by their green uniform jackets. They carried short-barreled muskets and short swords to facilitate their rapid movements during field operations. In general, Hessian Jägers were comparable to the troops of the British Light Infantry.

Normally, the infantry regiments consisted of 21 officers, 60 noncommissioned officers, 5 surgeons, 22 bandsmen, and 525 regulars. The grenadier battalions were each made up of 16 officers, 44 noncommissioned officers, 4 surgeons, 20 bandsmen, and 420 regulars. Each of the Jäger companies comprised 4 officers, 12 noncommissioned officers, 1 surgeon, 3 bandsmen, and 103 regulars, and each of the artillery companies accounted for 5 officers, 13 noncommissioned officers, a surgeon, 3 Bandsmen and 129 troops.

In most cases, the bands were staffed with oboe players (hautboists), pipers, drummers, trumpeters, and singers. Regimental staffs and other specialists included auditors, chaplains, quartermasters, provosts, advocate generals, as well as gunsmiths and laborers, i.e. wagon hands, wagon masters, and tent hands. It was also typical for a British or Hessian regiment to take along from fifty to eighty of their wives, who often served as nurses, laundresses, and shopkeepers.

A soldier's standard issue of clothing and equipment included a dark blue woolen jacket with facings in the regimental color, a waistcoat in the regimental color, a pair of white and a pair of black gaiters or leggings, two pair of white breeches, one pair of shoes, one red collar, an infantry sword, white belts for their sword, an ammunition pouch, and bread pouch, a backpack with white straps, a water bottle, a musket with red leather strap, and a tricornered hat with woolen tassel. Their hair were braided and tied in back, and every man carried a prayer book. The uniform jackets were cut small—especially the length of the sleeves—to make the wearer appear taller. In addition, grenadiers wore a miter cap with brass plate and carried four grenades each. It was typical for each man to have sixty rounds of ammunition. During their subsequent Atlantic crossing, every six men were issued a wooden spoon and a tin cup.

It was common practice at the time of the Revolutionary War to identify and associate the Hesse-Kassel units with the names of the regimental chief, perhaps the colonel in charge or even a prince or general. A regimental name could be altered whenever a new commander was assigned. On occasion, a regiment could hold the same name repeatedly, such as when a blood relative of an earlier commander took charge of the unit. Because of these practices it is often difficult to trace the lineage of Hessian units. (typical examples follow: the 1760 Regiment Wutgenau became the Landgraf Regiment in 1776; the 1759 Regiment Malsburg became known as Fusilier Regiment Lossberg in 1774; 1765 Regiment Knoblauch became Garrison Regiment von Huyn in 1774 etc.).

Following is a list of the Hesse-Kassel units committed to the service of King George III, showing their points of departure and initial marching dates:

Fusilier Regiment Du Corps (Leib Regiment) - Kassel - February 15, 1776

Fusilier Regiment Erb Prinz - Eschwege - March 2, 1776

Fusilier Regiment von Lossberg (Alt) - Rinteln - March 10, 1776

Fusilier Regiment von Knyphausen - Ziegenhain - March 3, 1776

Musketeer Regiment Prinz Carl - Hersfeld - January 21, 1776

Musketeer Regiment von Ditfurth - Marburg - February 11, 1776

Musketeer Regiment von Donop - Homburg - February 29, 1776

Musketeer Regiment von Trümbach - Grebenstein - March 4, 1776

Mobilization and Recruitment

Musketeer Regiment von Mirbach - Melsungen - March 1, 1776

Musketeer Regiment von Wutgenau (Landgraf) - Rheinfels - April 1776

Garrison Regiment von Wissenbach - Melsungen - May 7, 1776

Garrison Regiment von Huyn - Ziegenhain - Early May, 1776

Garrison Regiment von Bünau - Witzenhausen - May 9, 1776

Garrison Regiment von Stein - Harsfeld - May 6, 1776

Grenadier Regiment von Rall - Grebenstein - March 4, 1776

Grenadier Battalion von Linsingen - Wolfhagen/Immenhausen - early 1776

Grenadier Battalion von Block - Wolfhagen/Immenhausen - early 1776

Grenadier Battalion von Minnigerode - Wolfhagen/Immenhausen - early 1776

Grenadier Battalion von Koehler - Wolfhagen/Immenhausen - early 1776

Jäger Corps 1st Company - drawn from other units; augmented by volunteers;

Jäger Corps 2nd Company - Wolfhagen/Immenhausen - early 1776

Artillery (3 Companies) - various locations and step-off-dates

After the initial round of negotiations for troops had been completed, there followed additional bargaining sessions, most importantly for auxiliary troops from Ansbach-Bayreuth. That contract was executed on February 1, 1777. Several follow-on contracts for additional troops were also consummated with Hesse-Kassel and Hesse-Hanau. In October 1777 the final subsidy contract was signed with Anhalt-Zerbst. Under this agreement 1,119 troops were committed. Of these, one regiment served in Quebec and another contingent in New York.

Ansbach - Bayreuth Mobilization

Under the subsidy contract negotiated between Colonel William Faucitt and Carl Freiherr von Gemmingen, representing King George III and Margrave Christian Friedrich Carl Alexander, respectively, Ansbach-Bayreuth agreed to supply two regiments of Infantry, i.e. one from Ansbach and the other from Bayreuth, plus a

Captured color of an Ansbach-Bayreuth unit.
U.S. Army West Point Museum, West Point, New York

Company each of Jägers and Artillery. By agreement, 1,285 soldiers were to be supplied. By war's end that figure had risen to 2,353.

Each of the two infantry regiments consisted of a grenadier company and four musketeer companies, each with a staff of twenty-seven officers that included a chaplain, an auditor, a quartermaster, and a surgeon, plus 543 other ranks. The composition of the troops varied. Most officers were young and hailed from nobility. There were professional soldiers, but also many from lower walks of life as well as forcibly recruited personnel. People seeking adventure and others who were enticed by the idea of traveling were among the volunteers that joined up. Roughly one-third of all troops came from nearby states/principalities and were thus regarded as foreigners.

Based on his observations, the British negotiator assessed the troops of Margrave Carl Alexander as being well trained and equipped, and dressed in Frederician style, with uniforms cut the same as the Prussian army. In addition, the troops were said to be tall and well-built, in excellent condition, and that their weapons drills went off like clockwork. Although individual soldiers had no special or personal interest in the war overseas, they agreed for the most part that the Americans were rebels in that they rose up against the crown. Because of their rebellion, they were worth fighting. Still, the prince required unquestioned adherence to the Articles of War in order to maintain strict discipline. He made it the responsibility of the officers to set examples of proper behavior. Anyone guilty of desertion could expect the severest of punishments, unless the accused repented. Life and death were at the mercy of the Margrave; in the field that power was vested in designated regimental commanders.

Unit equipment included tents, assorted tools, canteens, pack saddles, as well as pack- and ammunition wagons. Besides their Prussian blue jackets, white trousers and vests, the men wore black knee-length gaiters. Uniform jackets of the Ansbach troops had red collars, sleeves and cuffs. The Bayreuth uniforms were trimmed in black. The soldiers were issued two pair of shoes, two pair of extra soles, and one pair of three-quarter- high boots. Also, a dress shirt plus two other shirts, one pair of linen pants, two neckties and hair ribbons. Drummers wore the same uniforms with vertical striped cloth wings added to the shoulders of their tunics to identify them as bandsmen. Musketeers carried a musket, bayonet, and cartridge and bread pouches.

The Ansbach Regiment was known as the First Regiment and was commanded by Colonel Freiherr August Valentin Voit von Salzburg. The Bayreuth Regiment, known as the Second Regiment, was commanded by Colonel Franz Johann Heinrich Wilhelm Christian von Seybothen after this regiment arrived in America.

CHAPTER 5

Troop Movements

THE OVERLAND TREKS

The logistics involved in the overland movement of the auxiliary troops from their home bases to the designated ports of embarkation required more than planning the respective cross-country marches. The need to secure permission from other sovereigns for entering and marching through their territories was often overlooked or not weighed in the planning process as potential obstacles.

The Brunswickers had assessed their own situation sufficiently to allow for moving the troops without any interference enroute. This was accomplished by sending the troops from Brunswick to their embarkation area at the mouth of the Elbe river via the British Crown's Electorate of Hanover. The troops from Hesse-Kassel were also able to proceed in a trouble-free manner, embarking their ships primarily at Bremerlehe (today Bremerhaven) where the Weser river enters the North Sea. The Waldeckers reached the North Sea by first crossing Hesse-Kassel territory and following the open routes north. Hesse-Hanau moved its troops by boat on the Main River and down the Rhine to Holland and their designated embarkation point. However, enroute they were stopped at Mainz on orders of the archbishop, who demanded that any of his citizens aboard the riverboats, including suspected deserters from his own army, be turned over to him. The British did not interfere with the archbishop's demands and protests by the troops' superiors fell on deaf ears. The riverboats were allowed to proceed only after the demands had been met.

The experience of the Ansbach Bayreuth regiments was of great

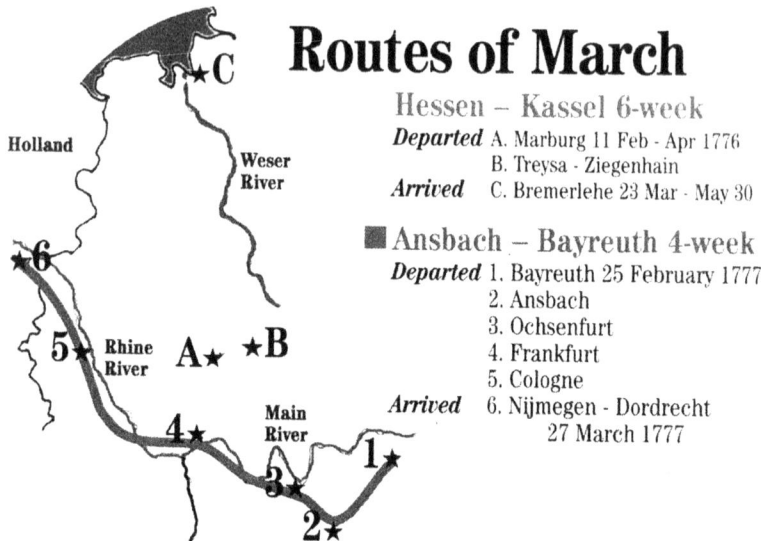

annoyance to the authorities, particularly since the personal intervention of Margrave Carl Alexander was eventually required. The 2nd Regiment marched from Bayreuth on February 25, 1777 to join up with the 1st Regiment in Ansbach. The combined corps of the two infantry regiments and a Jäger company then proceeded from Ansbach on March 7th, heading for the town of Ochsenfurt. On arrival at the Main River landing they were cheered by the local populace and welcomed with offerings of wine in plentiful quantity, which was enthusiastically received by the thirsty troops. The riverboats waiting to take the men onward appeared too small to the soldiers. Some panicked on the assumption they would be required to make the ocean crossing in them. In the meantime the wine kept flowing freely. While river transports had been ordered to accommodate some 1,400 troops and forty wagons loaded with equipment, there were actually 1,600 personnel on hand and ninety wagons that had to be moved downriver to the Rhine and onward to Holland for embarkation aboard larger ocean-going transports. These circumstances irritated the troops, who were becoming unruly. Even though additional river boats were made available, some of the troops chose to go back on shore. Calls for obedience went unheeded for the most part. The Ansbachers final-

TROOP MOVEMENTS

ly returned to their boats, but a Bayreuth contingent refused, ransacked a weapons cart, and headed into the hills and nearby vineyards. Jägers were ordered out to round up the deserters and return them to their assigned boats. There resulted an exchange of fire

Frederick the Great of Prussia. *Historischer Bilderdienst, Otto Quenstedt, Germany*

during the chase and several of the deserters were wounded. The group was brought back, though some 18–20 remained at large and were eventually picked up and shipped to America at a later date. Margrave Carl Alexander was notified of the situation and promptly headed for Ochsenfurt, arriving on horseback. He addressed his troops and reminded them of their commitments and responsibilities, succeeding in convincing them to continue on. Nevertheless, by the time the boats got underway, the margrave had made certain that the convoy route was secured from ashore by an escort of horse-mounted Hussars, who were to prevent any further desertions or disruptions of the task at hand.

Late in 1777, the Zerbst regiment was perhaps dealt the most severe of all blows when Prussia's King Frederick the Great announced he would prevent any troops destined for America from passing through his Prussian dominions. This resulted in the Zerbst regiment having to march through seven different jurisdictions and free cities. The inherent frustrations caused by the delays culminated in unexpected troop dissatisfaction and unruly behavior resulting in the desertion of 340 of the men. On-the-spot enlistment of some 100 fresh recruits helped to replace some of the deserters. The remaining contingent, though still below strength, finally made its way to Stade for embarkation.

Official as well as personal diaries and journals were maintained by Hessians and Ansbach-Bayreuthers in which they recorded the long marches to their embarkation points, and later also the hardships experienced while crossing the Atlantic Ocean on their way to North America. The following compilation of exerpts from several diaries, as recorded over a period of several weeks in 1776, provides an insight into the movement of the troops by land to destinations many hundreds of miles from their home bases, at a time when such distances could only be traversed on foot, or by waterway if such possibilities availed themselves along their selected route of march:

> We marched out of Ziegenhain on a beautiful day. Passing through Kassel, we paraded in review before His Highness... We departed to the sad lament of many people... Today we crossed the Weser River. At Bringsen we rode one hour through flood water... 150 wagons were ready to take us to the

Bremen border... we had the heavy baggage and field equipment unloaded from the riverboat... In a small village the field parson conducted services for the von Huyn Regiment in the local church at the request of the General... In a section of Brunswick we were being escorted by a patrol of mounted dragoons... We had good quarters and the people were nice... Next day we marched for five hours, then paraded with music in the city of Rodenberg... Some folks were saddened and wept for us; yet others cheered us on... Next day we marched for ten hours in gruesome heat... We had pancakes in the evening... When we marched onward, the townsfolk cried while following us to the end of town to bid us farewell... We were assigned to a poor and run-down village, a place we wished we would not have to stay in... Our wishes were soon fulfilled and we were moved to another locale and quartered there.

Embarkation

Overall, moving the various troop formations to their designated embarkation points over authorized land routes, through the countryside, and occasionally via certain waterways, required from four to six weeks from the time individual units stepped off, depending on the location of their respective home bases and whether or not they encountered any delays enroute. Judging from their staggered, yet fairly tight marching schedules, combined with the large numbers of foot soldiers originating from Hesse-Kassel, it may be anticipated there would have been some congestion on the preferred roads heading north. Though necessitated by treaty provisions, spreading out the marching dates had its benefits. It allowed the several regiments to complete any last-minute recruiting and gained them critical time to assemble needed supplies and equipment in anticipation of participating in an overseas campaign to which they had been committed by the sovereign. The staggered time schedule for the overland travel was also keyed to the scheduling of their subsequent onward movement via ocean-going conveyances. Due to the large numbers of troops involved and the limited number of ships immediately available to transport both all of the German-speaking auxiliaries and large numbers of British personnel, it became necessary to schedule their embarkation and sailing via two divisions, approximately one month apart.

As it played out, Lieutenant General Leopold Philip von Heister, under authority of Landgrave Friedrich II, took command of the First Division of Hessians, consisting of eight regiments plus two grenadier battalions, the Jägers, and an artillery company that sailed from Bremerlehe on April 17, 1776. His convoy initially sailed to Portsmouth, England, where it joined British troops aboard their transports and the men-of-war that would provide protection for the convoy. Heading out into the Atlantic they sailed the northern route to America, taking them close to Newfoundland and Nova Scotia on the way to their destination. From the time of departing Bremerlehe on April 17 and arriving at Sandy Hook, New Jersey, on August 11, 1776, more than three months had transpired.

The Second Division, under command of Lieutenant General Wilhelm Freyherr von Knyphausen, departed Ritzebüttel in June 1776, ultimately taking the southern route across the Atlantic, after they too had stopped at Portsmouth, England to join up with another British troop contingent and man-of-war escorts. Together, they formed another sizable convoy that finally sailed from England on July 20. This time, the planned sailing route would take them close to the Spanish coast and the Azores before crossing the open Atlantic to America. Knyphausen's Second Division comprised six Hessian regiments and two grenadier battalions, plus Jägers and troops from Waldeck. The Second Division arrived off Sandy Hook in mid-October.

Regimental Quartermaster G. Kleinschmidt, of Garrison Regiment von Huyn, one of the units embarked with the Second Division of Hessians, maintained the regimental journal. He enumerated the number of ships making up his convoy as being sixty-five, plus escorting frigates. Included in the lineup of the hulls were a hospital ship and five recruit transports. Kleinschmidt noted that every man was given a sheet, a small pillow, and a woolen blanket soon after boarding ship. Daily rations were said to consist of rice, peas, biscuits, salted pork and beef, butter, cheese, flour, a small ration of beer or rum, and water and vinegar for fumigation purposes. Allotted quantities of rations were distributed on a daily basis. Distribution among the troops was made in quantities to feed six men. A typical Sunday food allotment for six consisted of six pounds of biscuit or flour, six pounds of pork, three pints of peas, and eight gills or one quarter gallon of rum. Weekday rations for six always included six pounds of biscuit or flour, six pounds of pork or ten-and-one-half pounds of beef, two to four-and-one-half pints of peas or one and one-half pounds of rice, on some days also three-quarters of a pound of butter. While Kleinschmidt noted that the space allotted to the troops aboard ship was not too cramped, there are reports by others complaining of extremely tight living spaces. In good weather the men were expected to air out their bedding on deck and fumigate their living quarters with vinegar or tar, at the same time airing out the insides of the ship as much as possible. Time was also set aside for prayer during leisure times. Work parties from among the troops were designated to assist the sailors with their chores aboard ship, which could be particularly strenuous when it involved hoisting the anchor or moving heavy cargo and casks from the lower cargo holds. As appropriate, some ships were laden with horses and their feed, as well as artillery pieces and gunpowder. All types of equipment and supplies that would be required during a protracted period of time away from home had to be loaded, stashed, tied down, and taken along.

A diary kept by Johann Valentin Asteroth of Treysa mentions his transport having a capacity of 900 tons, with a length of 136 feet and width of 54 feet. He further observed larger ships in the fleet, including one with a displacement of 1,100 tons.

CHAPTER 6

Crossing the Big Divide

Considering that the voyage to America could be expected to take up to four months, description of such troop movements becomes of special interest to anyone attempting to place themselves in the position of the soldiers, since these men dealt with unexpected hardships and circumstances the likes of which they had not known before. Aside from the regulars and volunteers there were many conscripts among the auxiliarists, including young boys, students, peasants and even older men with little to no idea of what army life was—or could be—all about. Even to the regulars, the true professionals that had never taken a foot off solid ground, the overseas voyage presented many new challenges for which they had no rehearsed responses. Yet, for some a journey to America by whatever means promised to be the greatest adventure of their lives.

A better understanding of the 1776–1777 overseas troop movements can be gleaned from consulting the diaries that were maintained by the regiments and other independent observers at the times of their respective voyages. Composites of such data provide some detail of the challenges encountered.

FIRST DIVISION—NORTHERN ATLANTIC ROUTE—1776

The following information is taken from *The Journal of Regiment Ditfurth* (Dit) as supplemented or supported by information contained in the *Jeramias Kappes Diary* (Ka), an officer of Regiment von Knyphausen:

Regiment von Ditfurth.
Verein für hessische Geschichte und Landeskunde, Kassel, Germany

SAILED FROM BREMERLEHE TO PORTSMOUTH ON APRIL 17, 1776

April 17, 1776 (Dit) Cannon fired at 5:00 a.m. as signal to raise anchors. Ships got underway at 8:30 a.m. Good weather.

May 7, 8, and 9 (Ka) We had severe sea sickness.

May 13 (Ka) Around 6:00 p.m. one of our ship's lookouts fell from the middle mast and broke his arm.

May 21 (Ka) This morning around 9:00 a.m. a storm arose

Crossing the Big Divide

Colors for Regiment von Ditfurth.
Verein für hessische Geschichte und Landeskunde, Kassel, Germany

	which increased during the night so that we thought we would not see day again if God did not protect us.
May 22	(Ka) The storm continued. The sea was mountainous.
May 23	(Dit) Caught and prepared codfish, which appeared in great numbers.
	(Ka) The waves broke over the deck.

May 25	(Dit) Orders were given for the ships not to stay too close due to heavy winds and seas.
	(Ka) The ship's captain came in the evening with a carpenter and light to fix a leak down in the ship. We were very frightened and prayed to God for our lives.
May 26	(Dit) Waves unbelievably high and strong. Men often felt the ships would be smashed by the waves.
	(Ka) On this Pentecost day the storm increased.
May 27	(Dit) Ships were bounced to and fro that some men were even thrown from their bunks.
	(Ka) We still had the same storm. We were more sorrowful.
May 28	(Dit) We are witnessing the temper of the sea and its mighty size. Waves as high as towers on both sides. This ship's crew is no longer master. All is tied down and left to the mercy of the sea.
	(Ka) Same storm. We spent this Pentecost in great fear and danger.
May 29	(Ka) Same storm increased and we thought we would lose our lives to the wild sea. Toward evening God eased the stormy weather which made us happy and we thanked God for sparing our lives.
May 30	(Ka) Wind weak. Convoy collected itself again, but the *Malaga* was missing. A man-of-war was sent to look for the missing one. We saw many large fish seven feet long and four wide.
June 1	(Ka) The ships raised flags as it was the King's birthday and the men-of-war fired salutes with their cannon which was nice to watch.
June 10	(Ka) We passed a meridian. Our sailors who had not passed this line before were baptized with salt water and each one had to pay for a half measure of brandy.
June 16	(Ka) We saw a sailor from the ship *Spring* fall from

	the mast into the sea and drown.
June 21	(Ka) Very heavy fog. We were separated from the convoy by fog and sailed on alone, arriving on the Great Banks of Newfoundland.
June 24	(Ka) Today, on St. Johann's Day, it was so cold we could not remain on deck. Every evening we provide thirty men for deck watch. Man-of-war *Cygnet* returned to its station on the fish banks.
July 3	(Ka) The fog was so heavy, a ship collided with us and placed us in great danger as we thought we would sink. By evening fourteen of our ships were together.
July 5	(Ka) This morning the anchor was raised and with God's protection we arrived in Halifax harbor. The city is only twenty-six years old and growing constantly, but the houses are built of boards.
July 7	(Dit) Earlier orders to head for Rhode Island were changed. Fleet would head for Sandy Hook instead.
	(Ka) Around 12 noon we again met our convoy. The war ships saluted with many cannon shots.
July 10	(Ka) Around 3 o'clock such a wind came up that we thought the storm would tear off all the ship's sails. It abated in the course of two hours.
July 30	(Ka) We had a full-blown storm. Land was sighted but the storm forced us seaward.
August 2	(Ka) Good wind; sailed six miles per hour. In the afternoon there arose such a storm that we were placed in danger of our lives.
August 6	(Dit) To our delight we found bottom today; white sand, calm sea and very hot.
August 11	(Dit) We saw green grass that floated from land with the tides. By evening land came into view.
August 12	(Dit) Sighted Sandy Hook and a light tower built of stone that was displaying the British flag. We had been enroute for fourteen weeks. A large fleet of

twenty-seven sails greeted us with fire from thirty cannon. Several ships ran up on sand bars as they entered the bay, but were able to clear the obstacles without damage. Anchored off Staten Island in the afternoon where we were greeted with many gun salutes by the fleet of Admiral Howe.

(Ka) Under God's protection we sailed past the lighthouse into New York harbor. The same day we dropped anchor twice.

August 14 (Dit) Debarked at Staten Island

August 15 (Ka) Under God's protection and help we were debarked. We were on the ship *Mermaid* from April 15 to August 15, four entire months. We were laden on Staten Island and camped near the water.

SECOND DIVISION—SOUTHERN ATLANTIC ROUTE—1776

The following information is taken from *The Journal of Garrison Regiment von Huyn* (vH) as supplemented or supported by information contained in the *Diaries of Chaplain Heinrich Kümmel* (Kü), and *Johann Valentin Asteroth* (Ast), both of whom were associated with the von Huyn Regiment.

SAILED FROM RITZBÜTTEL TO PORTSMOUTH ON JUNE 28, 1776

June 28, 1776 (vH) We weighed anchor; the fleet had increased to sixty-five ships.

(Ast) Our transport ships totaled seventy-two. Four war ships escorted us.

July 14 (Kü) We were disembarked from the uncomfortable ship *Five Sisters* and transferred to General Schmidt's ship, *Four Good Friends* where nearly three companies of the von Huyn Regiment were to be found.

July 20 (vH) We set sail (at Portsmouth) on a signal given by our Commander.

July 28 (vH) We whiled away the tedious hours in conversation and reading books; porpoises rolling about. Fishes, so-called Portuguese man-of-war, poison-

Garrison Regiment von Huyn.
Verein für hessische Geschichte und Landeskunde, Kassel, Germany

ous and the size of a small ship afforded us enjoyment to watch.

(Kü) We left the English Channel near Lands End.

August 5 (Ast) Terrible storm in the evening. Sailors secured the sails and tied everything down, leaving the ship to maneuver at will. Thirty bunks that had been rigged in three tiers for six men each, collapsed. God the Almighty saved us.

August 16	(vH) It was the honored birthday of his Serene Highness our Gracious Sovereign, and with much gratification we celebrated the same.
August 20	(Kü) We passed among the Azores islands of St. Michael, Maria, and Flores, and the great mountain of Pico.
August 21	(vH) The length of the voyage caused us to grow impatient. There was great homesickness, we grew tired of sitting, standing or lying down.
September 7	(vH) A sudden whirlwind, which they called a hurricane.
September 10	(vH) The transport *Adamant* with the Waldeck troops aboard, was on fire. Lt. Colonel Lange of the von Stein Regiment was buried at sea.
September 12	(vH) Dolphins chasing fish; high seas. Ship rolling: no fires allowed; no hot food.
	(Ast) Our war ships captured a Rebel ship with a crew of ninety men and twelve cannons.
September 26	(vH) Corporal Conrad Schmeer died; simple ceremony, his body was sewn in two blankets, weighed down and slowly lowered into the water.
September 28	(Kü) A small privateer ship was captured and taken with us.
October 2	(Kü) We had such a good wind that we sailed 210 miles in a twenty-four-hour period.
October 16	(vH) Land sighted; called Block Island.
October 17	(vH) Anchored between Staten and Long Island.
October 20	(vH) On to New York harbor.
	(Ast) Anchored off New York. Debarked at New Rochelle. First time on land after twenty-two weeks.

VOYAGE OF THE ANSBACH-BAYREUTH REGIMENTS—1777

Having restored order among his troops after the March 10, 1777 Ochsenfurt mutiny, Margrave Carl Alexander made it a point to accompany them all the way to Nijmegen, where Colonel William Faucitt, the British emissary was waiting to receive them. After he swore in the troops to serve the King of Britain, the Margrave returned to Ansbach. Over the next two days the regiments moved on to Dordrecht near the border of Holland where they boarded larger ships for their voyage to America. The 620 troops from Bayreuth were accompanied by twenty-nine of their wives, since married soldiers were allowed to bring their spouses with them. There was fear among the troops at some 115 men being crowded into the transports along with supplies and provisions, and then being at the mercy of rough and ill-mannered sailors. Their convoy to England got underway on March 29, 1777, but had a layover of several days in Portsmouth, to allow several other transports to join them. During this time, some of the soldiers were permitted to disembark and visit the city. Their convoy of seventeen ships, including a single warship for their protection, finally commenced the voyage across the big divide.

Although the Ansbach-Bayreuthers sailed the preferred southern route via the Azores, their experiences on the high seas were no better than those recorded by the Hessians during the prior year. Hardships enroute must have been overwhelming. As with the earlier convoys there were casualties to report, including a case of suicide. The convoy bringing the Ansbach-Bayreuth regiments to America after an eight-week voyage, finally reached New York and Staten Island on June 3, 1777.

OTHER IMPRESSIONS

There exist several descriptions of conditions aboard ship that are more critical and go beyond what has been described. Such comments may be found in letters sent home as opposed to what might appear in the journals of record. Men feel at greater liberty to speak freely when communicating with their own, rather than when documenting events in unit histories and the like. On the other hand the discontented are more prone to be critical of almost anything.

One case involves a report by Johann Gottfried Seume, a poet who was involuntarily impressed into service despite rules forbidding such practices. He complains that tall men could not stand upright between the low decks and that six soldiers had to squeeze into a berthing space intended for four personnel. His description of the food is extremely critical, describing the beef and pork as being discolored and several years old. Biscuits were often full of maggots despite the fact they were so hard that one needed a cannon ball to break them to pieces. He surmised the biscuits had been taken from the French during the Seven Years' War some twenty or so years earlier, now to be fed to the Hessians. Water casks when opened stank and water had to be filtered before drinking.

In a letter to his brother, an unidentified Hessian soldier serving on Rhode Island included comments to this effect:

> Motion sickness was unbearable and discomforts indescribable; no one who only half knows the discomforts would ever dream of taking a trip to America. Ill because of bad food; old hard bread, stale water stinking like a barnyard puddle, smelly butter and musty peas. Constant dangers: a ship barely missed running into his ship, which in turn almost hit another ship; One ship hit his ship's anchor and damaged part of its upper deck. Waves were as high as the crow's nest. After a storm, some of the sails, part of the upper deck and several mast ropes were missing. Two recruits died aboard ship, and one child was born.

The voyages across the big waters took many weeks. For the ground troops totally inexperienced with sea travel and the ways of the Atlantic Ocean, the excessively long time aboard ship brought about many fears, especially during the heavy storms over which neither they nor their sea captains had any control whatsoever. Not only did high waves engulf their ships, but the masses of salt water breaking over the decks spilled into the inner decks and down to the lower level troops compartments, drenching their uniforms and bedding, and leaving everything soggy and musty smelling. Mold soon developed among their possessions. Despite all of these irritations, there were also many long and dreary days without any meaningful activity except to watch the sea, endless in nature with nothing in view but open sky and an empty horizon. Tensions combined with sea- and home-sickness at times brought on short tempers and depression fanning arguments and flare-ups that prompted serious confrontations from time to time. Duels aboard ship were not unheard of although they very seldom took place. In addition to the listed troubles and inconveniences the troops had to contend with the presence of rats in the holds that fed on the already scarce food supplies. General von Riedesel became so upset and frustrated at conditions aboard ship and the long voyage that he vented his inner feelings in a letter in which he referred to the ships' crew as pigs, scoundrels, and ruffians.

CHAPTER 7

America

Following their disembarkation on Staten Island, several hundred men who had fallen ill enroute were soon given required medical attention. It is of note that some of the others who had weathered the crossing without too much difficulty took sick in the early days after planting their feet on solid ground once again. It is assumed that the switch from the unsatisfactory fare aboard ship to a healthier and more regulated diet produced some unexpected ill effects. Under the agreements reached with the King earlier, Hessian soldiers were treated by their own Hessian doctors, and if hospitalization was required they were to be admitted to a facility operated by Hessian medical personnel.

Even though individual soldiers had no personal stake or interest in the war, many did perceive the colonists as being unlawful and traitorous rebels who dared seek to dethrone their king. Following their arrival in America, the conditions they observed quickly confused the soldiers, in particular when drawing comparisons between the Americans with their many possessions, and their own families who were living simple lives in Germany. They considered the colonists to be living in luxury, with almost everyone owning a home and a piece of land for farming through which they could trade for the essentials of life. Why such people with such an abundance of wealth would want to revolt was beyond the comprehension of the ordinary soldier who was being sent by the crown to put down the uprising.

On the military side, there seemed to be considerable equality among British and Hessian troops, and they got along with each other pretty well. Lower-ranking Hessian officers up to the regimental commanders could operate in relative independence of any British influence in smaller operations. The Hessian military hierarchy, while being highly respected and praised openly, did not fare as well. They were caught in a struggle of rivalry with their British counterparts. Although the Hessian assessments of situations and their recommendations were heard, the British High Command in the end proceeded as it saw fit, often without commenting or giving notice to the top Hessian commanders. This situation was not appreciated by Lieutenant General von Heister, then the top Hessian commander on the continent who criticized Britain's General Lord Howe for being indecisive. Upset, Lord Howe communicated with his own superiors in Britain and succeeded in orchestrating the relief and return to Europe of General von Heister in July 1777. Following his departure, Lieutenant General von Knyphausen assumed command of all Hessian forces. His methods and tactics in dealing with the British soon earned their respect and they eventually accepted his military advice to some degree.

Landing of English troops in New York.
From an engraving by Francois Xavier Habermann.

NEW YORK

Even before disembarking at Staten Island, diary notes were being penned recording the respective writers' first impressions of the city called New York. One entry noted that New York was large and very well situated. Senior Auditor Motz stated in part that it is a pleasure to the eye seeing New York from aboard ship. He spoke of so-called bridges (piers) that reached far into the sea so oceangoing ships could tie up to them and unload their cargo without having to bring their goods ashore via small boats while the cargo ships remained at anchor farther out in the bay. Both he and other diarists made mention of having observed wide streets, some even tree lined, and some houses that were beautiful in appearance, especially those built of stone with large balconies. The steeples of at least two churches were seen from a distance, but also 2,000 or more small one-story houses that had been made of wood, which one writer assessed as being badly built.

As might be expected, once inside the city the young Hessians quickly took note of the beautiful women. Soldier Johann Asteroth noted that the women were slender and well built without being plump. He described their skin as being very white and observed that they had a healthy complexion with no need to paint themselves. He also noted that hardly any had pock marks on their faces. He was impressed with their manners and secure bearing, commenting that the women cared much about cleanliness and good shoes. Even the way they combed their hair was of interest to him. Asteroth mentioned they curled their hair every day and tied it into a knot in the back of their head, then brought it forward into a raised position. He didn't miss the few "country nymphs," as he called them, who let their hair hang loose and used a headband instead. And while their houses looked poorly built the people lived well, with the women wearing coats and gloves when they went out. This young soldier was so impressed with the fine appearance of the American women that he planned on taking time whenever possible just to stand and look.

DUTY CALLS

Not long after the landing operations on Staten Island had been completed, Sir William Howe prepared to attack the enemy, directing his attention toward Long Island. When the assault commenced on August 22, 1776, British and Hessian troops landed unopposed and quickly made their way to Flatbush. After the battle, General Heister observed that the rebels had offered considerable opposition to the British, but quickly surrendered out of fear after spotting the blue coats of the Hessians. The foregoing notwithstanding, there were continuing skirmishes over a period of days during which additional Hessian troops were brought ashore. By August 27, British and Hessian troops had essentially outflanked the vastly outnumbered rebel forces on Long Island and succeeded in taking many prisoners. The others retreated to prepared positions in Brooklyn and from there, at night and taking advantage of the fog, George Washington moved them across the East River to New York Island (Manhattan).

On September 15, 1776, Lord Howe managed to invade Manhattan under the protection of a number of warships. His forces landed in the Hell Gate area and in part between Kips Bay and Bushwick. Resistance was offered by a brigade-sized unit of Washington's men that had taken up positions behind stone walls. A Hessian grenadier battalion was engaged to attack and dislodge the rebel force. The assigned task was accomplished after the grenadiers had suffered many dead and wounded. The enemy then retreated behind its lines in the vicinity of Fort Washington.

British and Hessian units with drums beating and flags waving, marched into New York City with only a few apprehensive onlookers taking note of them as they paraded through the streets. While some British observers reported the troops being enthusiastically received by the population, there are indications that the two Howe brothers were disappointed in the lack of support shown.

Although the British command anticipated that the rebels would torch New York to coincide with their landing in order to reduce its value to the invaders, this did not take place at the time expected. However, four days later a tremendous fire erupted in the highly populated area of New York that burned for almost two full days. There are reports telling of a quarter to a third of all houses in the city being lost to the fire; others set the number of houses destroyed at 1,100 including a Lutheran church and Trinity Church. Despite a possible delay in any planned torching, official sources on both sides seemed certain that the fire was attributable to patriot action.

However, Lossing's *Pictorial Field Book of the Revolution* provides a report by David Grim, a New York merchant who witnessed the inferno. He claims "the fire broke out in a low groggery and brothel, a wooden building on the wharf near Whitehall slip." Grim delineates the area of the fire in which all buildings were consumed by the flames as being bounded by Whitehall, Broad, and Beaver Streets, then expanding toward Broadway and burning houses on both sides as far as Exchange Street. In its path, the fire consumed Trinity Church. This report set the number of buildings destroyed at 493 out of a total of 4,000 buildings that made up the city at that time. The devastated area was later repopulated by utilizing remaining walls and chimneys and adding wooden supports and old ship's canvases to create huts and tents as substitute shelters. For some time thereafter this area was dubbed Canvas Town, where "the vilest of the army and Tory refugees congregated."

Fort Washington in New York and Fort Lee, across the Hudson in New Jersey, were part of George Washington's line of defense and guardians over his lines of supply and communication across the Hudson. Because Fort Washington was of such great importance to the rebels, a joint British-Hessian attack was soon launched on November 16, 1776, with the Hessian force being lead by Lieutenant General von Knyphausen. After overcoming a number of obstacles, the attackers moved forward swiftly with other regiments following in support. These forces included some of the newly arrived troops of the Second Division, who had been quickly added to the advancing forces to help overwhelm the enemy at Fort Washington. The onslaught forced the defenders to surrender. Some 2,600 prisoners were taken and large quantities of supplies and weapons captured. Across the Hudson, Fort Lee was given up and later taken by British General Cornwallis. Effective November 21, 1776, Fort Washington was renamed Fort Knyphausen. These were indeed glorious days for the Hessians and the King's men.

The joy of the early victories was shattered on December 26, 1776 when Hessian forces at Trenton, under command of Colonel von Rall, were caught off guard in a surprise attack by General Washington's men. This followed on the heels of a severe snow storm during which the Hessians had sought shelter. Washington's epic crossing of the Delaware was followed by an ensuing two-hour melee in which, thirty Hessian soldiers were killed and 918 of the 1,400 men at Trenton were captured. Colonel von Rall was badly wounded while attempting to rally his troops. A few hours after surrendering his sword to General George Washington, he died of his wounds. Many of the remaining Hessians fled to Bordentown, New Jersey. On hearing of the lost engagement at Trenton, the local commander ordered the evacuation of Bordentown, to the dismay of his superiors. Among the troops captured by Washington's forces were the Regiments von Rall, von Lossberg, and von Knyphausen, artillery and grenadier units, and the Jäger corps. This engagement became the first substantial defeat the Hessians suffered, and fifteen of their flags that would normally have been proudly carried into battle were lost.

The Trenton affair occured when General Clinton's expeditionary forces in Newport and Rhode Island were still getting organized and acclimated to their newly assigned area of responsibility. Among the troops that had been put ashore in Newport on December 8, 1776 were some of the more seasoned Hessian regiments that had played decisive roles in the victories at White Plains and Fort Washington.

CHAPTER 8

Newport

Perhaps one of the most interesting descriptions of colonial Newport can be found in the diary of Captain Friedrich von der Malsburg, officer of Regiment von Ditfurth, and commanding officer of the First Company of Chasseurs. This officer not only managed to compile a detailed record of his observations in and around Newport, he also made special efforts to document current events and describes with much detail features of the city that impressed him as being unique. Many of his comrades were similarly impressed as they wandered about the streets of Newport in their spare time, but it was Malsburg who took the quill in hand to compile this lengthy record. In so doing he not only created a personal diary but a truly unique description of events and places for the benefit of posterity.

SOCIAL MATTERS AND VIPS

The following translated excerpts for the month of December 1776 provide an insight into the social life of the military during the occupation of Newport:

Wednesday, December 18
Major General Prescott was elevated to the position of Commandant and Lieutenant Colonel Campbell of the British 22nd Regiment was made Commandant of the city.

Thursday, December 19
After removal of the plates, the table cloth was removed and all sorts of wine in bottles were brought on. Many "toasts" followed, for health of the King, the Queen, the Royal family, the Landgrave, the Brothers Howe and the success of their

Captain Friedrich von der Malsburg of the von Ditfurth Regiment, and commanding officer of the First Company of Chasseurs in Newport in 1776–1779. *Courtesy Gero von der Malsburg, Germany*

weapons. The Lord proposed all the toasts and when done, asked each of the gentlemen present to propose a toast for a loved one. Thereafter, there was conversation during which time coffee and tea was served.

Saturday, December 21
...In evening, at request of Lord Percy: rehearsal at Crown Coffee House for a concert with 30 voices...

Sunday, December 22
Returned courtesy of my neighbor Mr. Newton, by inviting him for lunch. Attended dinner with Lord Percy's Lord Rawdon and other English officers that was given in the quarters of Hessian Brigade Major Wallenberger. The music of the Second Hessian Regiment's Band was well received. Had an opportunity to meet Miss Bardin, the beautiful daughter of the house and several of her friends who had been invited.

Wednesday, December 25
Christmas Day. All ships decorated with flags. Invited by Captain Jillard on board the *Tryals*. Visited Goat Island with its strong stone fort that can hold forty-two cannon. It has several barracks and good casemates. Previously known as Fort George, the rebels changed its name to Fort Liberty. This was spelled out in large letters on a tin sign fastened to a pole in the center of the fort. At the retreat of the enemy only six cannon were left behind.

Thursday, December 26
Order received that members from any Regiment or Corps are forbidden to take anything considered "Rebel property" without special permission. Promised a concert for Monday. As a result, was introduced to some of the most fashionable houses and was very well received. In the evening completed our engagement and attended a concert and dinner at the home of doctor Destailleur of the English Artillery.

Sunday, December 30
We drilled in very cold weather. At noon I had the company of English officers, all of whom enjoyed music. In the evening the first ball was held in the large hall of the library. I was surprised to see such fashions among the residents and a large group of attractive ladies. It is said that most of them were

Excerpt from Capt. von der Malsburg's Diary.
Staatsarchiv Marburg, 10E Kriegstagebücher I, NR 1 18-1/2 BI-1-8I

Tories. A good time was had... The revolution is one of the most evil and sad circumstances.

MALSBURG'S DESCRIPTION OF NEWPORT

The city is situated at 41 degrees and 30 minutes North; has from 1,000 to 1,200 houses, mostly of wood and sandstone that are two to three stories high. A number of very nice buildings with Italian roofs stand out and reflect the well-being of their owners. The interiors are normal and moderate. Downstairs near the entrance are usually the rooms called parlor, and dining and drawing rooms. The first is the living room of the owner, the second the dining room, and the third, the visitation room. The families' living spaces and bedrooms are upstairs. The kitchen is in the back end of the house. The quarters of the slaves and the stables are in the yard. At the farthest point away in the yard are the toilet facilities in nicely-built little houses. The buildings in this neighborhood have a front yard enclosed by an iron picket fence and six to eight stone steps leading to the house. The furniture is of mahogany throughout; the richer have furniture of more expensive pimento. All are artistically crafted. All floors are covered with very colorful carpets and every room has a sofa. Tapestry of cotton and calico are not well known. The rooms have a pleasant and lively appearance with picture hangings on the walls. In the center is a fireplace with needed tools of polished iron and decorated with the finest brass. In some houses silver is used. Above the fireplace is the mantelpiece decorated with bronze urns or figurines. Mirrors are on both sides as well as two wall sconces. Next, there is a wall closet on each side which serves as storage for wood on the bottom and above it is used as a sideboard. A stranger entering such a visitation room on a winter's night can only be impressed by its air of grandeur with the sight of six or seven burning logs in full flame. The fireplaces are lined inside with black marble or a similar material and have a protective plate in front made of perforated steel or brass to contain the sparks of the coal from blowing into the room. Whenever coal or ash falls out, the tools kept in readiness are used to sweep it all back into the fire. The family sits around the fireplace, always ready to host their friends.

This description is but of the first houses; they are not any less comfortable than those of the more wealthy. The doors are locked. The door knocker need only be heard and a slave will open the door. Cleanliness is the mark of this well being and of good fortune; it provides much for the slaves to do. These negroes also hold such positions as servants, stable hands, and maids.

Europeans who arrive without money are indebted to the sea captains and must work to pay off their passage. Since they are mostly received well by the colonists, their's is a tolerable situation. When their debts are paid off, their masters will give them some money or an advance. Thereafter they will settle and build, and have the same rights as citizens of the state.

The city is built on a hill facing the sea. Except for a few, the streets are not paved. Thames or Main Street that runs along the harbor in a straight north south line for a half mile is well paved. There are only a few public buildings.

The library (built in 1747), in the form of a Greek temple with four pillars in front, is made of stone blocks and is very attractive. It is in an elevated position and dignified, making it

Redwood Library, from a 1768 pencil sketch by Pierre Eugene Du Simitiere. The library was the site of occasional social events during the British and Hessian occupation. *Library Company of Philadelphia*

appealing to the eye. It houses several thousand volumes, which I have just learned are unprotected since the librarian left at the onset of trouble.

The Court or Town House is a large building of sandstone. It stands above the parade ground and the spaces once used to preach revolution now serve as our main guard station...

The Colony House in Newport was used as the Guard House for the British-Hessian garrison. *The Newport Historical Society*

...several religious buildings with preachers still there; crowded on Sundays. Then there are two Presbyterian churches of good construction and appearance (referred to as Congregational or Puritan). However, since the preachers traded guns for their bibles and most of their congregations followed their example, one was taken to serve sick soldiers and the other for services of the garrison. A Jewish synagogue is a massive and new and graceful structure. Regret that it is in a hidden place where it cannot be seen too well. There are several other churches here: Baptist, Anabaptist, Quaker, Moravian, and assembly places of a few sects. The harbor is safe against all winds, with a capacity of receiving 1,000 ships. It is considered the best for this part of the world. From the center to the end of Thames Street and the section called Point Bridge, ship wharves are situated close to the houses, making it easy to load and unload cargo.

Erich A. O'D Taylor, author of *Campaign in Rhode Island MDCCLXXVIII*, noted "the town fraternity of masons is not out of sympathy with their brothers in the army. On St. John's Day a joint picnic among British and American members was held in the lot near the library."

THE FEAR OF THE HESSIANS

No matter where the Hessians were assigned they were always viewed with fear, perhaps even as barbarians, at least until the colonists got to know them better. Some sources describe them as presenting a terrifying, if not fierce appearance with their high brass caps, black mustaches, and serious countenances. It is understandable that negative reports about the Hessians would have been even further exaggerated by the rebel propagandists during the war to turn the population against them. It is also known that some ministers participated in the call for resistance against the crown, which did not improve the general attitude against the Hessians. Part of this fear may also have resulted from the earlier Hessian victories in the New York area, where they gave no quarter. Once victorious, some of the soldiers resorted to plundering, which was pretty much accepted as a routine occurrence in those days. German historians point out, however, that the pay of some troops had been delayed for over two months and that the lack of currency to supplement their meager rations drove them to steal. It may also be presumed there were some who carried the plundering too far. In consideration of the prevailing circumstances, von der Malsburg resolved in 1776 that he would maintain the strongest discipline against plundering among his men in order to win the trust of the civilian population. Later in the war he received plaudits from the people of Newport for his efforts.

The deep-rooted fear of the Hessians by Newport's Quakers is expressed in Lieutenant MacKenzie's diary notes for December 13, 1776: "...A Quaker told me today, that as the rebels were now driven off the island, he hoped the General would send all Hessians on board the ships again."

Seduction of Hessian Troops

In an effort to encourage Hessian desertions, the American Congress, on August 27, 1776, in a resolution signed by John Hancock, President of the Continental Congress, invited all foreigners in the military service of His Majesty to leave his service and become American citizens. Land grants were promised free and clear to those electing to come over to the American side, with acreage proportioned in accordance with their military rank. To take advantage of this offer anyone planning to participate would have to do so before the offer is withdrawn.

Under this resolution, colonels would receive 1,000 acres, lieutenant colonels 800 acres, majors 600 acres, captains 400 acres, lieutenants 300 acres, ensigns 200 acres, noncommissioned officers 100 acres, and others would be awarded acreage in keeping with their rank and pay status. Any officer bringing others with him could expect additional rewards. In addition to the foregoing rewards the participants would be permitted to practice their own religion and have all the rights and freedoms as other inhabitants of the land.

Initially, the Germans showed little interest in the bribes offered. However, the shortage of food and encouragement by the civilian population in due course resulted in numerous desertions from among the Hessian ranks. Anyone apprehended in the act of deserting could expect harsh punishment, usually the running of the painful gauntlet. On the other hand, several deserters apprehended during the British-Hessian occupation of Newport were sentenced to death by hanging.

CHAPTER 9

Soldiering in Snow and Ice

THE CLOSE OF 1776

In light of the extreme winter weather during the days following their landings in Newport and Middletown, both British and Hessian units were speedily assigned to permanent winter quarters in the town of Newport. At the same time, other units were deployed throughout the countryside in an effort to adequately secure all of Aquidneck Island which was at that time referred to as Rhode Island. Early reconnaissance, according to Lieutenant MacKenzie, determined that "the rebels have a fort on their side of Howland's Ferry (Fort Barton), and (that) they also have some pieces of cannon on a height above it, by which means they entirely command the passage, for the ground on our side, called Commenfence Neck, is flat land.... which extends near a mile from any part where we can establish a post." He further noted that "they have a fort and battery also on their side of Bristol Ferry... and fire occasionally at any person who appears within their reach." Based on his recorded observations the enemy appeared to be well established across the narrow waterways at the northern end of the island.

Captain von der Malsburg noted that substantial numbers of British troops were being quartered in the city of Newport as of December 16, 1776, but also that several of the frigates that had accompanied their convoy from New York were being deployed and stationed all around the island. Four of the warships operating within the bay were posted on both sides of Prudence Island to effectively blockade the estimated 70–80 enemy ships that were believed to be further up the bay in Providence, thus denying them

Many Thames Street homes served the British and Hessian troops as winter quarters. *Author's photo*

access to the Atlantic.

Aside from routine military duties and operations, the need for firewood was soon placed high on the agenda of essential functions to be performed. Accordingly, on December 20, a detail of 200 British and Hessian troops was dispatched to Shelter Island with six transports, tasked with cutting and gathering firewood and transporting it to the Newport garrison. This assignment, being the first in a series of similar incursions into unfamiliar territory, was of sufficient import at the time to have been mentioned in both British and Hessian diaries. The scarcity of firewood, coal, and light prompted the establishment of a system of rationing and distribution.

Under the date of December 25, 1776, the *Journal of Regiment von Huyn* lists the following allocations:

> A Brigadier received two cords of wood weekly, a Colonel 1-1/2, a Lieutenant Colonel and Major 1. A Captain 1/2; a Subaltern 1/4, and a cord for every 12 men. One pound of candles was reckoned to each 1/2 cord of wood, and 12 bushels of coal to one cord of wood. A cord was as much as 1-1/4 yards, and one bushel was equal to two packs."

When word was received on December 21 that a large corps was being assembled in Providence by the enemy with plans to attack the island, a number of defensive actions were immediately taken. A battery at the northern end of the town was put on alert, as was the staff at the main guard station within the town. Two cannons were drawn up at that station to fire garrison-wide alert warnings should the need arise. Concurrently, the chasseurs who had been posted in Portsmouth until this time were moved to Brenton's Neck, while others were engaged in setting up signal torches at various locations across the island. The construction of earthworks also got underway at Windmill Hill (called Butts Hill by the Americans) and at Fogland Ferry. At the same time orders were issued to report any unusual happenings to the commanding general.

A report was received on December 23, to the effect that enemy pirates had taken valuable goods from a British ship that had been earmarked for the troops. Anticipating that the rogue ship might not be aware of the British presence and decide to land in Newport, the soldiers at the Brenton's Neck fortification were alerted and instructed to hoist an American flag upon the sighting of any foreign ships. It was hoped this deception would mislead the robbers sufficiently to come ashore, at which time they could be apprehended.

Lieutenant MacKenzie next reports on a boat manned by a lieutenant and five men from a rebel privateer of ten guns that came ashore at Brenton's Neck on December 28. They were immediately seized by the troops quartered there and brought to headquarters. Captain von der Malsburg, in reporting this incident, noted that a detail of Hessian chasseurs had remained concealed until the group disembarked and then captured them.

A news report that appeared soon after the above events spoke of a captured American naval lieutenant from an alleged pirate ship who had been beaten by General Prescott or some other senior officer, despite standing orders issued by Lord Percy forbidding the mistreatment of prisoners. Whether the alleged improper treatment is linked to either of the foregoing events cannot be ascertained.

So that religious services could be conducted, the garrison in Newport was assigned the Presbyterian Church (possibly

Congregational or Puritan) that had been abandoned by its clergy and overseers. On Sunday, December 29, 1776, the first services were held at that site for British and Hessian personnel. Because of the large turnout, Lord Percy thanked von der Malsburg repeatedly for the arrangements that had been made despite the extremely cold winter weather.

INTENTIONS VERSUS REALITY

Lord Howe, in ordering the occupation of Newport by a large military force certainly wanted to establish a strong foothold on Rhode Island after abandoning Boston and leaving it to the rebels. In assessing the pros and cons of the area, he considered Newport and its vicinity the perfect place for his majesty's troops to rest up after their long and often dangerous voyages across the Atlantic, as well as for those who had already been in battle for a period of time.

Disembarking the troops at the height of what turned out to be an extremely cold and unpleasant winter, however, did not fit the good intentions of granting them a well-earned period of rest and relaxation, even if only for a short period of time. One might imagine what the soldiers' reactions might have been at having to sleep on frozen ground during that first night ashore, and in flimsy tents for a period thereafter before being assigned to more sturdy shelters, i.e. houses abandoned by residents who had fled rather than live under the guns of foreign troops. As barren and cold as these houses may have been at first without the furnishings prior owners had taken with them when they departed the premises, living within solid walls during the days of high winds and drifting snow would soon have been accepted by the soldiers as a bonus, if not a luxury. These conditions notwithstanding, social events and gatherings of the top British and Hessian leadership were not allowed to suffer.

The harsh weather and other personal inconveniences aside, the troops quickly became aware that the enemy was nearby and that they were, in effect, isolated and surrounded by hostile forces. They learned of their isolation from their own experiences and observations while patrolling the island and from the activities of unfriendly ships within the bay. And all this occured within the first three weeks of their arrival in this strange land far from home. In this environment the men in the field had almost daily encounters with small American details that crossed over from Tiverton to ambush or harass the isolated British and Hessian outposts that had been established at the northern end of the island, some five hours marching time from their Newport garrison.

At times the rebels would succeed in capturing sentinels and carrying them off, or would provide likely deserters an opportunity to leave the service of the King. Some intruders made quick landings for the purpose of plundering. Hessian and British patrols would engage them on sight or following the receipt of reports from the population.

One consolation to the Hessian soldiers and their British allies was that the deep waters around the island served as a natural barrier similar to the moats of old, making Newport and the island reasonably defendable, except perhaps for the incursion of smaller groups at isolated locations in the countryside. Coping with larger enemy forces was not necessarily foreseen at that time; only time would tell if Newport and the island could be successfully defended in such an eventuality.

For the moment, the main concern of the British was the rebel force said to be gathering in Providence and any possible force that might attempt a landing from the direction of Bristol or Tiverton, or perhaps even from the mainland to the west via Conanicut Island. To forestall the latter possibility, troops had been detailed to secure Conanicut Island as soon as Clinton's armada had landed in Newport. Occupying Conanicut Island with a strong troop contingent would contribute to keeping the main passage of Narragansett Bay open and under British control, simultaneously preventing rebel shipping, known to be trapped in Providence, from exiting the bay for open waters.

Finally, on December 31, several rebel ships coming from Providence made an unsuccessful attempt at running the British blockade that was being maintained in the lower bay area. A lively cannonade ensued before the ships were forced to turn back—an event that for all intents and purposes signaled the end of 1776.

It had been an exceptionally eventful year for the Hessians who were here on orders of their prince; and another year was about to begin. What might it bring?

CHAPTER 10

1777—A Time of Quiet?

TROOP DISPOSITIONS

Summarizing the first quarter of 1777, Christoph Wende, Quartermaster of the Ditfurth Regiment, made the following entry in the regimental journal:

> The garrison spent the entire winter in the quiet of their winter quarters with little more than routine garrison duties. In mid-May we received orders to prepare for a move to an encampment site.

If this entry were taken at face value it would appear that all had been quiet in Newport and Rhode Island for the duration of the winter months. Quartermaster Wende, however, could speak only for his own regiment, one of three that had been housed within the town during that period, the other two being the DuCorps Leib Regiment and the Prinz Carl Musketeer Regiment. The above three regiments formed a brigade under Colonels Lossberg and von Bose. The three remaining Hessian regiments were assigned billeting outside the town with many of the men experiencing their first American winter in tents or other hastily constructed shelters. These units occupied the northernmost outposts on Rhode Island, grouped into a separate brigade under Colonel von Huyn, which comprised the Regiments von Wutgenau, von Bünau, and von Huyn. The *Journal of Regiment von Huyn* describes their winter duty assignment at the northern part of the island, which by no means could be interpreted as having been quiet. It reads in part:

> ...They frequently attacked our detachments and made several attempts to land, so that several times, especially during the night, signals were given by firing guns and setting alarm

poles on fire for the regiments to turn out immediately. But every time they found the enemy quite brisk and who at all times thwarted their designs and drove them back again...

The Ditfurth Regiment moved out of the town to replace the von Wutgenau Regiment that had been encamped behind Windmill Hill, not far from their patrol area between Common Fence Neck and westward to an area just opposite Bristol. These troop movements appear to have been routinely accomplished. At the same time, considerable hostile action was being encountered on the waters of the bay, disproving the notion that this period in early 1777 could have been considered a time of leisure and relaxation. It was certainly not for the British naval elements on patrol, nor for the gunners manning their cannon at various strategic points in and about the town of Newport and along the shore of Narragansett Bay.

DISAPPOINTMENTS

In this regard it is noteworthy that the *Bayreuther Zeitungen* reported *H.M.S. Diamond*, a British frigate, being stranded at low tide off Warwick Neck in early January 1777 and being fired on for about three hours by five rebel twenty-four-pounders. Listing to one side, the *H.M.S. Diamond* could respond with only two of her onboard cannon. Two crew members were killed during the incident and, the hull of the ship was pierced seven times below the water line and its sails damaged. The stated misfortune notwithstanding, the ship was able to dislodge itself after the change of tide, in time to get under way before an approaching "swarm" of enemy boats could reach its position.

Local troop morale was struck a severe blow when a packet ship arrived in Newport on January 2, relaying the sad news that Colonel Rall had been surprised by Washington's militia at Trenton, New Jersey, on December 26, resulting in the capture of his entire brigade, which included the Regiments von Knyphausen, von Lossberg, and von Rall. A lack of attention during the Christmas season contributed to this unexpected loss of manpower, and it dealt a terrible blow to the prestige of the Hessians. Considering the success they scored at Trenton, the Americans might become more brazen and daring in future operations—good reasons to be alert at all times. When he received word sometime later, the Landgrave

1777—A Time of Quiet?

was so infuriated that he demanded a full investigation into the conduct of each of the officers involved. In addition, the regiments that had lost their flags as a result of this shameful event were not to be issued new colors until the units had once again distinguished themselves.

By mid-month there had been several attacks on British ships within the Bay by land-based American gun batteries. Likewise, British ships were continuing their blockade of the passage to Providence and engaging enemy shipping wherever possible.

Matters of Command

On January 13, 1777, Sir Henry Clinton left for England, handing over command of the Newport garrison to Lieutenant General Lord Hugh Percy, who until that time had served as the deputy commander. The latter remained in charge until he too departed on May 5, at which time Major General Prescott assumed control over all British and Hessian forces in the Newport and Rhode Island area of operations.

In a letter dated March 31, 1777, Captain Klingender of the Ditfurth Regiment forwarded a communication to his superior, Lieutenant General von Ditfurth in Hesse, that had been received on Rhode Island by Colonel Lossberg. The letter originated at Headquarters Tyverton under the date of February 21, 1777 and was reportedly signed: "Warnum." In it, the originator explained and justified the actions of the colonists and asked what interests and rights the Hessians had in America; that all men were brothers and from the same father originally, and that Britain's sparkling gold and intrigues had deceived the Hessians. He continued by saying that all, save a few bad men, loved them dearly, yet his own people were being called rebels, etc. It must be assumed that Captain Klingender's letter with the noted enclosure would have been mailed to Hesse via the first packet ship sailing for Europe. Considering the time inherent in moving the correspondence by boat from Newport to New York, then to England and onward to Germany, at least eight or more weeks would have transpired. Formulating an appropriate response—if one were appropriate—would have taken additional time to which would have to be added the time needed to deliver the reply to Newport. It is doubtful that any meaningful response could have been generated by Lieutenant

General von Ditfurth, considering that his superior, the Landgrave, had committed the troops to the service of Britain's King by way of contracts beneficial to his own interests.

TROOP REDUCTIONS

Despite the almost daily skirmishes at the north end of the island and the continued sparing among the ships on the bay, the British high command apparently felt satisfied that it could securely maintain its presence on Rhode Island and defend the town of Newport with fewer troops than assigned at the time. Besides, additional manpower was sorely needed elsewhere, particularly after the loss of the three Hessian regiments at Trenton. There was a need to fill the void resulting from their capture. Accordingly, the British 63rd Regiment and Hessian Regiments DuCorps and Prince Carl were directed on May 6, 1777 to prepare for embarkation. Quartermaster Kleinschmidt of the von Huyn Regiment was alerted to proceed to New York with the others to reconcile and balance the 1776 accounts of the remaining four Hessian regiments. Quartermaster Wende of the Ditfurth Regiment apparently accompanied Kleinschmidt since his regimental journal shows he had dealings with British paymaster Mollinsworth in New York about the same time for the purpose of picking up the payroll for Regiments Landgraf (Wutgenau), von Ditfurth, von Huyn, and von Bünau.

The alerted troops embarked on May 18, but were delayed one day in sailing for New York due to the heavy fog that blanketed Narragansett Bay. As they waited aboard ship for the fog to clear, they were passed by two boats containing sixty chasseurs and their officers on their way to Conanicut Island, where they were to relieve the British 54th Regiment.

The *Bayreuther Zeitungen*, reporting on activities of May 26, 1777, notes that the von Bünau and von Huyn Regiments had left their winter encampments and moved to Newport to secure the harbor. The reporter is quoted as follows:

> At this time we can hardly tell a war is going on; we don't see or hear the enemy and our encampment near the water is comfortable. Food stuffs are expensive, but anything can be had for money – which is not scarce. The inhabitants of the city come to our camp with all kinds of goods for sale.

1777—A Time of Quiet?

The *Bayreuther Zeitungen* also noted that the ship *Unicorn* had brought in a rebel ship loaded with sugar and rum. It went on to say that the *Unicorn* had captured a total of twenty-one ships, bringing eleven of them into the harbor of Newport; that the *Unicorn* had escorted the reporter's convoy from Europe, and that it was said to be the fastest ship in the entire fleet.

The Prescott Kidnapping

The event most disturbing to both British and Hessians alike was the kidnapping and capture of their top Commander, General Prescott, on July 9, 1777. The Continentals, who assembled in the area of Tiverton Heights as early as December 1776 when the combined British-Hessian forces landed on Rhode Island, anticipated they would at some time in the future occupy the north end of the island. The shortest route to that objective would be via Howlands Ferry in Tiverton. Early actions on their part included building a fort at Tiverton Heights from where the narrow passage could be readily observed and taken under fire. Fort Tiverton Heights was commissioned on June 28.

Soon after, on July 9, Colonel William Barton picked forty of his best men for a special mission. The group first made its way to Warwick Point. Proceeding from there at 9 p.m. in four or five whale boats, they headed for the western shore of Portsmouth, disembarking at Coddington's Cove in the dark. They next followed a small stream that passed near the home of Mr. Overing, a Quaker, that was situated on West Road where British General Prescott was known to be staying most of the time.

An entry in the *Journal of the Ditfurth Regiment* for July 10, 1777 provides the following details:

> Last night we lost our Commanding General Prescott. He had his house four miles to the rear of the front near the west side of the island. A guard detail of six men maintained one sentry near his quarters, the rest were at their post a quarter of a mile away. A rebel troop coming from the bay made its way past the men-of-war that were at anchor in Narragansett Bay. They overpowered the guard and found both the General and his Adjutant, Capt Barrington, sleeping. A Dragoon assigned to the General became aware of the happenings and made

enough noise to cause the Regiments to move out, however, nothing was found by the time they arrived.

General Prescott was taken prisoner and transported to Providence, where he was treated well and permitted to move about rather freely. In the days following, some of his belongings were delivered to him under a flag of truce. He was later exchanged for the American General Charles Lee, who had been captured in New Jersey by the British. Exchanging prisoners of equal rank was an accepted practice in the eighteenth century, and it was expect-

On July 10, 1777, British General Prescott was kidnapped from the Overing House by a detail of forty men under the command of Colonel Barton. *From B.J. Lossing's Pictorial Field Book of the Revolution.*

ed that the exchanged prisoners would return to duty and take up arms once again.

Soon after, the fortification at Tiverton Heights was named Fort Barton in honor of Colonel Barton's daring and highly successful raid.

CHANGE-OF-COMMAND

On July 21, British Major General Pigot arrived from New York and was met by a Hessian honor guard of thirty men at the Newport docks. Pigot had been recently promoted to the rank of major general for gallantry and was known to be a good administrator, well-fitted to command the Newport garrison. Within the first few days of his arrival, Major General Pigot made it a point to visit and inspect the outposts at the north end of the island to familiarize himself firsthand with the situation, the lay of the land, and the disposition of the entrenched enemy across the narrow passage. Although the most essential defensive positions had been built or were under construction by British and Hessian work details, a more aggressive program all across the island and beyond got underway soon after Major General Pigot completed his assessment of the overall defensive posture of his newly-assigned command in the Narragansett Bay area. In due course he was able to increase the number of troops under his command by adding the Franconian Ansbach-Bayreuth Regiments, the British 38th, and a supporting artillery unit to the Newport garrison.

CHAPTER 11

Troop Administration

STAFF FUNCTIONS

Hessian regimental staffs included certain special ranks, in particular a Quartermaster, an Auditor, a Chaplain, a Provost, an Advocate, and also, at times, a Surgeon.

THE QUARTERMASTER was perhaps the best known because of his responsibility to secure housing, equipment, and food supplies for the troops. His was a sizable job considering the constant transfer of units from their permanent quarters in town, to temporary facilities in the field, and their subsequent return after completion of a period of service at remote sites.

THE AUDITOR was the chief accountant and overseer of finances. In Newport, Quartermaster Wende of the von Ditfurth Regiment functioned as paymaster for his own as well as for the von Bünau and von Huyn Regiments, an additional duty for which he was given extra pay. The Franconian troops had a similar arrangement. It is interesting to note certain differences in the administration of the Hessians' pay vis-a-vis Ansbach-Bayreuth personnel. Although both served under the same conditions and circumstances, the Ansbach-Bayreuth contingents received their full pay while a portion was withheld from the Hessians' income, to be disbursed upon their return home. Some soldiers elected to have a part of their pay sent to their families.

THE SURGEON operated the hospital, where he was assisted by medical personnel and some of the soldier's wives who served as nurses. In February 1777, orders were issued preventing British and Hessian surgeons from inoculating anyone with smallpox. For health and cleanliness reasons, troops were forbidden to transport or carry coal, bread, and other items in their bedsheets. In early 1779, a time when food supplies were in short supply in Newport, some soldiers scrounged up anything they could lay their hands on that looked edible. Several of these men gathered locoweed and cooked other poisonous roots and ate them. They soon became deathly ill, some losing their sight and hearing. Milk was the apparent antidote; still, one died from this unauthorized brew. In addition to such unexpected situations, the hospital staff was tasked with handling any battle casualties and illnesses that would impact troop capabilities and morale.

Losses because of sickness and epidemics required a constant flow of replacements from home. A shipment of Ansbach-Bayreuth replacements and recruits left their families the end of October 1777. The 318 soldiers had sailed up the Rhine to Bonn, where they were denied onward passage through Prussian territory. Frederick the Great, uncle of Margrave Alexander, would not weaken in his resolve to prevent the Franconian replacements from entering or passing through his domain. This refusal was upsetting to the Margrave. However, the replacements he had promised the King of Britain were nevertheless required to march from the Rhine River area all the way across Germany to Bremerlehe on the North Sea in order to board their transports. They finally shipped out on May 6, 1778, arriving in New York at the beginning of September, and in Newport on October 12th.

THE CHAPLAINS were considered conscientious in providing their services to the troops who sought their advice when troubled by earthly circumstances—evidence that religion had a strong influence on these men. Each had been issued a prayer book, and Sunday service was a part of their regular duty. Troops would march to their respective churches, wearing their full dress uniforms and ammunition pouches, and carrying their weapons. Chaplain Heinrich Kümmel, who was quartered with a Baptist minister, serviced several of the Hessian units in Newport, while Chaplain Johann Phillip Erb ministered to the Ansbach-Bayreuth Regiment. Since the Presbyterian Church had been abandoned by its clergy and overseers it was assigned to the Newport garrison for religious services. Chaplain Erb gave his sermons in the Quaker Meeting Houses in Portsmouth and Newport. He also conducted

Troop Administration

services in the field at times when the men were unable to leave their positions and provided special care to the members of the congregation whom he visited as needed.

Among their music and songs during the Revolutionary War was Martin Luther's hymn: "Eine feste Burg ist unser Gott," (A mighty fortress is our God). Other songs popluar at the time included: "Ein Schifflein sah ich fahren..." (A ship I saw a-sailing), "Prinz Eugen," and "O König von Preußen" (Oh, King of Prussia).

Many church buildings in town had been abandoned and were taken over by the British and Hessians for use as billets and hospital facilities. Captain von der Malsburg noted the existence of a Jewish Synagogue, describing it as "a massive and graceful structure." He also mentioned various other active religious communities in Newport including Baptists, Anabaptists, Quakers, and several unspecified sects. Trinity Church was the only house of worship that had not been seized by the occupying forces due to its relationship with the Church of England. It also served as the garrison church for British troops during their Sunday church parades.

Most of the Hessian and Franconian troops were Protestant. The principalities Ansbach and Bayreuth had become Protestant about 1530 by decree of the Margrave. There were some Catholics in their ranks, but they are said to have been among those recruited from "foreign" lands such as Bohemia.

The chaplains kept meticulous records, documenting with considerable detail the clerical services they rendered, listing by name and date all births, baptisms, marriages, deaths, and those receiving communion or being counseled. Several births, baptisms, and infant deaths were recorded at the Windmill Hill encampment in Portsmouth, which verifies that the wives of some of the men had accompanied their husbands even on their field assignments.

THE PROVOST AND THE ADVOCATE were the enforcers and upholders of discipline and the laws prescribed by their prince. In addition to being routinely disseminated among the ranks, certain orders of the command were also publicized in the *Newport Gazette*, a weekly newspaper published for the British occupation forces. All of the higher-ranking British officers at one time or other made insertions in the paper addressing certain pet annoyances. Such was the case of General Prescott, who frowned upon the dispensing of spirits

Trinity Church was used as the garrison church by British troops who used it for Sunday church parade. *Rhode Island Historical Society*

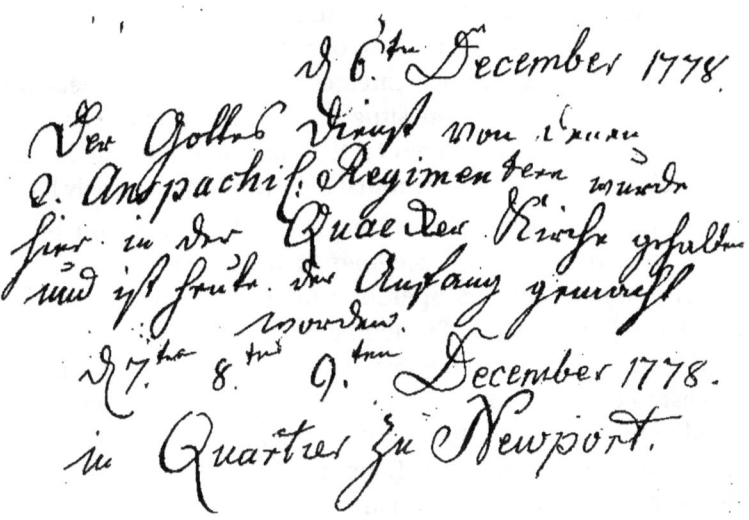

Lt. Johann Ernst Prechtel of the Ansbach Regiment recorded his regiment's church services at the Quaker Church on December 6, 1778.
The Huntington Library, San Marino, CA

without a license, and Major General Pigot who forbade private rum sales to the troops. Usually, punishment was associated with noncompliance.

Judge Metcalf Bowler of Portsmouth is said to have petitioned General Clinton in early December 1776 to provide a guard for his home in Portsmouth to thwart Hessian pilfering. (Note: Bowler was believed to have been a leading colonial patriot until the 1930s when it was discovered he had actually been a paid British spy).

At about the same time Captain von der Malsburg resolved to maintain the strictest discipline against plundering, in an effort to win the trust of the civilian population. He apparently succeeded. Both he and General von Huyn received testimonials from the inhabitants of Newport at a later date, thanking them for their extra efforts in maintaining discipline among their troops.

Although the Hessians in British service in America are said to have been the best-paid soldiers in the world, with some even able to save money to send home to their families, they were always tempted to desert to the enemy. The Americans offered farms and citizenship that could be acquired through marriage or by fathering an American child. These enticements sounded very tempting to young men in a foreign land an ocean away from home, except for the fact that their prince threatened potential deserters with death by hanging. There were situations where repentent deserters could be pardoned, but in general the punishment handed out by the Hessians for any type of criminal behavior was extremely harsh.

Court-martials were held in Newport periodically with British officers conducting the proceedings in cases involving their own subjects. Hessian officers operating under the mandate of their own prince judged cases of potential wrongdoing by their soldiers and the women under their jurisdiction. Women could be jailed for one year or be sent home if their presence in the theater was determined to be detrimental to the troops. Illegal marriages were punishable by flogging; the colonel's permission was required before a soldier could marry a local woman.

During the period of British-Hessian occupation of Newport relatively few judgments of death by hanging were handed down. The sentences were normally carried out in the presence of Hessian troops. Both Hessians and British personnel were among those executed.

Lt. Johann Prechtel noted that common soldier Schmidt was punished to run a gauntlet of 200 men twelve times for having stolen money from a store. *The Huntington Library, San Marino, CA*

Lieutenant MacKenzie's reports, the *Journal of Garrison Regiment von Huyn*, the *Journal of Regiment von Bünau*, and the diary notes of Lieutenant Prechtel of the Ansbach Regiment together provide a fair insight into how crime were addressed, particularly among the Hessians and Ansbach-Bayreuth troops:

There appears to have been an increase in the number of desertions among the Hessians and Franconians during the month of August 1778—more than in any other month. In excess of twelve men sought to desert during that time and two were recaptured. Perhaps the heightened anxiety and expectation of being crushed between French and American forces prompted the men to take irrational steps.

Lashings and running the dreaded gauntlet were common punishments that were doled out to violators. The following information is compiled from the above cited records:

Punishment Day: two men ran gauntlet; one eight times for attacking a guard; the other, ten times for disrespect.

A common soldier stole 1 1/4 Spanish dollars from a store. Punishment: Run gauntlet of 200 men twelve times.

A common soldier stole gunpowder at Goat Island and a 24-lb cannonball. Punishment: Run gauntlet of switches twenty four times in two days.

A private who had deserted was captured. Because of his young age, instead of suffering death he was punished to run a gauntlet of 200 men, thirty-six times in two days.

A negro cut the ears off a provisions horse. Punishment: 250 lashes.

Two men attacked a Royal Marine. Punishment: Run gauntlet fourteen times.

Soldier found another soldier's purse and kept it. Punishment: Run gauntlet eight times.

FRATERNIZATION AND MARRIAGE

Social events and socializing in general were part of the life of the British and Hessian garrison in Newport. Spending time with the locals, in particular the families of Tories were normal occurrences.

One case stands out, however, because one of the officers

involved acted inappropriately and was later arrested. The culprit was Captain Christian T.S. Molitor, who had been promoted to company commander in the Bayreuth Regiment on April 16, 1778. Coming from deployment in Philadelphia, he arrived in Newport on July 16th, along with other members of his regiment. As far as is known he apparently discharged his duties properly at all times. Following his later return to New York in 1779 as part of the overall evacuation of Rhode Island by the occupation forces, he married a young American lady named Rebecca Engs, without obtaining prior permission. This omission resulted in his arrest in 1783.

Molitor's wife, Rebecca, was one of the daughters of Quaker merchant William Engs of Newport, with whom both British and Hessian personnel socialized. Katherine Engs, sister of Rebecca, had married British transport Captain Drummond in July 1778 and went to live in London with her husband. Another sister, Mary, married Captain Georg Vultejus of the Hessian von Ditfurth Regiment and moved to Hesse when he returned home. Upset at having been placed under arrest, Molitor asked to be discharged. His request was granted and he set out with a group of his followers for Nova Scotia where he received a 700-acre land grant and lived for a number of years. Both he and his wife were later buried in their new country.

HESSIAN RECORDKEEPING

The regimental documentation pertaining to their respective units is worthy of special mention. A review of the *Monthly Reports of the Colonel von Bünau Regiment* for the period August 1778 through October 1778 provides insight into the thoroughness with which the regiment accounted for the whereabouts and condition of each of its men.

One might compare the variety of data collected and recorded as approximating the military morning reports of our day, except that it was documented in longhand by the Hessians. The reports were formatted as spreadsheets identifying the several regimental units followed by columnar entries giving numbers of their personnel present as well as the numbers and whereabouts of those absent or no longer to be accounted for because of transfer, hospitalization (in Newport or New York), desertion, or death. Special notes were made documenting the rank and names of the men wounded and the extent of their injuries. Promotions and demotions were also made a matter of the monthly reports as well as any transfers of personnel in and out of the unit during a given period. Date-of-Rank rosters listing both officers and common soldiers were appended periodically to the monthly reports.

CHAPTER 12

British Defensive Measures

Early Colonial Actions

Soon after the confrontation at Lexington between British forces and the colonists in the spring of 1775, which resulted in the first action of open warfare, Brigadier General Esek Hopkins of the Newport Company of Militia began to prepare defensive breastworks in Newport, utilizing 300 of his troops for that purpose. In due course additional works got underway, including Tonomy Hill in Newport as well as at other more distant sites in the countryside, such as Butts Hill, where crude earthworks were started. By January 1776, some nine months after Hopkins' first defensive construction projects had begun, the colonists realized the day was drawing closer when they would have to defend themselves actively against the British. Conanicut Island, because of its favorable location at the entrance to Narragansett Bay, would likewise need to be fortified. For this reason, Brigadier General Hopkins and an entourage of 300 troops were detailed to the island, tasked with building a fort at Beavertail sufficient to receive six or eight cannon. Similar projects were concurrently executed by militia units in localities facing the bay as far north as Providence, and in Tiverton on the Sakonnet River.

Accession of Conanicut Island Resources

Among the first actions taken immediately following the December 7, 1776 landings of British and Hessian forces at Newport was to secure Conanicut Island. For this purpose, a detail of 100 men from the British 54th regiment was dispatched to the island on December 12, with the balance of the regiment following on December 19. These troops took possession of the earthworks originally built by the Americans under Esek Hopkins on the west side of the island. While there, they were quartered in nearby houses. Dumplings Battery, also on the island, was of great interest because of its strategic location on the channel facing Newport. Besides its desirable location at the entrance to Narragansett Bay, Conanicut Island was a great source of wood and forage to the occupying forces.

One German diarist noted that Conanicut Island became known as "Hay Island," since it was especially well suited for producing hay. Because of this essential resource there was a constant rotation of troops from Newport to the island. Several times during 1777 combined British-Hessian work details were on the island. Hessian diaries show that their chasseurs spent some time on Conanicut Island the same year and that they were replaced by members of the von Huyn Brigade. In July, a work detail consisting of one man from each British and Hessian Battalion was sent to the island to make hay. A forage magazine was established near the ferry landing and kept under guard by an assigned detail. It was estimated at the time that Conanicut Island could produce approximately 1,000 tons of hay. Overall, General Howe was seeking ways to acquire double that amount to meet his planning needs.

Information contained in the MacKenzie diary, and supplemented by entries in certain monthly reports of the von Bünau Regiment, show that eighteen whaleboats coming from the mainland and carrying 150 men landed on Conanicut Island on August 3, 1777, with an unconfirmed mission to burn the hay magazine. Men carrying rakes surprised a guard of the von Bünau Regiment near the shoreline and carried him off. A second guard alerted other nearby Hessians, who fired at the landing party and forced their hasty withdrawal from the island. Valentin Asteroth, a soldier of the von Huyn Regiment, noted in his diary that the von Bünau troops on Conanicut Island fired at the approaching rebels from their "defenses" with cannon and small arms. MacKenzie reports that several of the rebels were unable to return to their boats before they cast off, forcing them to throw away their arms and attempt to save themselves by swimming to Dutch Island, which was quite a distance away. Pertinent monthly reports of the von Bünau Regiment show that "Common Soldier Christian Thomas was captured on Conanicut Island on August 3rd, 1777." This notation was carried forward from month-to-month. It was further reported that the above-mentioned group of colonists had landed on Dutch Island, where they were said to have stolen some sheep before proceeding to Conanicut Island. There they succeeded in capturing the Hessian guard before being forced to abandon whatever plans their detail of 150 men may have had.

It is said that two storage areas for firewood were established near the lighthouse on Conanicut Island, but that rebels had set them on fire twice. As a consequence, a wood storage yard was set up in Newport. Because there never seemed to be enough wood on hand to satisfy the needs of the combined British-Hessian garrisons, old houses and parts of the wooden wharves eventually found their way to the piles of firewood. In light of their incessant demand for burning materials, the British are known to also have burned the pews from churches they had confiscated for use as barracks. In due course many trees around the island fell to the ax, and even wooden fences were used to keep the troops warm.

BRITISH ACCESSIONS AND EXPANSION IN NEWPORT

As might be expected, all of the breastworks and fortifications abandoned by the colonial militia were promptly recycled or modified to fit the immediate needs of the occupying troops. During the Spring of 1777 the earthworks begun earlier in Newport by Esek Hopkins and his men were expanded by British and Hessian work crews. A line of defensive positions was laid out and prepared from Green End northward on high ground and then in a westerly direction toward Tonomy Hill. General Pigot is credited for perfecting the island's land defenses and eventually extending the defensive positions to Coddington Point (a high knoll at the edge of the Bay) and adding more breastworks along the general line of defenses. A considerable amount of effort went into preparing Tonomy Hill as a citadel armed with heavy guns. At the same time, details were at work building a redoubt in the vicinity of the three windmills that were located on the north side of Newport in those days.

North Point or North Battery, often referred to as Fort Greene, was originally built by the citizens of Rhode Island in 1776. Located on the shoreline of Narragansett Bay and southwest of Tonomy Hill, it was armed with a number of eighteen- and twenty-four- pounder guns. From here, the colonists successfully drove the British ships *Scarborough* with twenty guns, and *Cimetar* with eighteen guns from their anchorage off Rose Island in April 1776. The ships moved closer to Conanicut Island from where they were later forced out to sea by the guns emplaced at the Dumplings, Brenton's Point, and Castle Hill. As with all other sites they captured, the British confiscated North Battery, putting it to good use two years later when the French Fleet entered the Bay in support of rebel objectives to dislodge the combined British-Hessian garrison from Newport.

DISAPPOINTMENTS ON BOTH SIDES

In early September 1777, the British ship *Juno* put a detail of men ashore on Prudence Island in two boats to fetch water. They were attacked by 100 rebels, who killed two of them and captured eight others. Additional British seamen and marines from the *Juno* rushed ashore to give chase, but the enemy had retreated. In gathering up the dead it was found that one of their men had been stabbed with a bayonet in several places and shot through the head three times. This infuriated the British, who swore to avenge these barbarous acts.

In 1777, General Spencer was in command of Rhode Island troops, i.e. Militia and Continentals. A plan he devised to dislodge the Army of Occupation from the island of Rhode Island and Newport was well received. In October, after assembling some 9,000 troops across the waters of Rhode Island's north end, ready to invade the occupied island, it was determined there was an insufficient number of boats on hand to ferry the troops across. A severe storm complicated the situation even further. These unexpected circumstances required the invasion plans to be scrapped, much to Spencer's chagrin. As commander of the aborted operation he was personally blamed for the lack of more detailed planning which gave rise to such great a failure. In the wake of this disappointing experience he lost his command in December and he was later court-martialled. General John Sullivan of New Hampshire assumed his duties soon after.

Captain von der Malsburg, in a letter of January 3, 1778, written to his "Noble Baron and Gracious Lieutenant General" from a redoubt at Foglands Ferry commented on the above failed plan of attack, as follows:

I informed your Excellency of the hostile attack which a body of 15,000 men under General Spencer intended making on this island, but they desisted from their plan after continually menacing us for five weeks. We hear now, that the reason for this was because General Palmer's Brigade did not assemble early enough. As I was uncertain what the result would have been owing to our dangerous position, we were not disappointed that nothing came of the attack. The sight of 300 flatboats just opposite the place where I was positioned with my Corps of Jägers and the probability of it being their landing place caused me to offer as much resistance to their plan as possible, in consequence of which I and my men have frequently spent the whole night lying on our stomachs near the riverbank on watch for the enemy. The construction of four hostile batteries opposite me and the ship, and the differing preparations they were making for the attack, all of which went on before my eyes, required all of my attention. Consequently the anxiety I suffered during that portion of five weeks was unavaoidably proportionate to the importance of my post, and it was impossible for me to sleep at night. I once had a man of the Landgrave Regiment killed and another wounded, owing to my camp being constantly bombarded, so I was obliged to leave it and seat myself somewhere behind a hill...

In order to expedite the work at several sites in the town of Portsmouth, General Pigot on September 13, 1777, summoned all able-bodied civilians to report for work on a number of redoubts under construction in their neighborhood. On September 15, only seventeen showed up at the designated time. Most of the men reporting were Quakers, whose beliefs prevented them from assisting the war effort in any manner, not even in supporting roles such as building earthworks. Despite this setback and the shortage of manual labor, work on fortifying the north end of the island, i.e. the Portsmouth region, continued unabated, and mostly with troop labor.

Later in October, after word had been received of the surrender of General Burgoyne's army at Saratoga, there was considerable concern in Newport that the rebels might now be in a position to free-up forces sufficient to carry out an attack on Newport in the not-too-distant future. This reality contributed to a new round of orders to expedite the completion of the various defensive works. About the same time MacKenzie noted that "a great many disaffected persons have been taken up in Newport and sent on board the prison ship." He felt it was time to confine them, as they had been expressing their sentiments too freely. Because of this contentiousness, there was no doubt that they would engage in actions contrary to the best interests of the British in the event of an attack.

PROJECTS GO FORWARD

According to MacKenzie, the troops were busy fortifying different posts on the island; additional defensive positions had been planned, and others were already traced out. However, he could not envision how all of these projects could be completed by December. The projects at the north end were centered on Windmill Hill (Butts Hill), about eight and one-half miles north of Newport. British documents of December 31, 1777 show a battery of six guns and a redoubt for 100 men having been prepared on the hill as of that date. Also, a separate barracks for 300 men and officers had been erected in close proximity to the other. The entire area encompassed earthworks some 700 feet long by 200–300 feet in width. Abbatis—an entanglement of cut tree limbs serving a role similar to barbed wire in modern times—had been placed outside the entrenchments and earthworks to slow down and harass advancing enemy foot soldiers. Abbatis were also a part of the construction effort at other fortified sites. The list of redoubts that were actively being worked on by Hessian and British troops included Barrington Hill, a facility for eighty men and two cannon, with an artillery park to the east of West Main Road at Lehigh Hill; Quaker Hill, with a building capable of housing 200 troops; and Turkey Hill, with barracks for sixty men. Earthworks were also thrown up at Anthony Hill, at the west end of Lawton's Valley, at the Glen near Middletown's Third Beach, and at Fogland Ferry.

The overall effort to establish a tight net of defensive strong points also included sites in the Middletown area. Among these was Fort Fanning, a large fort near West Main Road at Two-mile Corner, and Green End Fort (known as Card's redoubt), an expansive earthworks at Bliss Hill opposite Honeyman's Hill Road, which

British Plan of Works at Windmill Hill (Butts Hill).
Pierce Collection Portsmouth Library, RI

was situated at the eastern end of the British line of defenses. In due course many of the cherished fruit trees at these sites were cut down to clear the view of the defenders, while at the same time creating impassible abbatis from entanglements of tree branches around the various earthworks. Houses that obstructed the

Corner section of Butts Hill with view toward Tiverton Heights.
Taken from Edward Fields' Revolutionary Defences in Rhode Island

defenders' field of view were also knocked down in this process. In one instance all cattle and corn were seized from a farm from whose owner had left with the rebels and the house was ransacked by Hessian soldiers and then, demolished. These actions, though of a defensive necessity to the occupiers, were viewed with considerable consternation by the population, in particular by those citizens who were directly impacted. At the same time, some 180 loyal inhabitants of Newport volunteered to serve the occupation forces. Once signed up under so-called "Articles of Association," they were organized into three companies and assigned patrol duties within the confines of the town of Newport.

An additional inner line of defenses was established around Newport proper in the following year. Essentially, it paralleled the earlier line of fortified strong points, except that it was much closer to and partially within the populated area of Newport. It was designed to serve as a last line of resistance should the garrison be hemmed in by the enemy. In setting up the outer, as well as the inner line of defenses, a field of considerable depth had been created and cleared to the detriment of the advancing enemy, while at the same time providing prepared fallback positions for defending troops. The effectiveness and theory of the system would have to be proven.

Despite the heavy and accelerated construction effort put forth by the combined British-Hessian garrison, routine administrative matters took their normal course. So it was that orders were received by mail boat on October 18, 1777, promoting Colonel Lossberg of the Leib Regiment to brigade general. Colonel Bose was at the same time promoted to general of the Landgrave Regiment. Lossberg immediately moved into the city to assume command of all Hessian troops in Newport and elsewhere on Rhode Island.

CHAPTER 13

Raids and Incursions

OFF-ISLAND ASSIGNMENTS AND HAPPENINGS

As noted earlier, the critical shortage of burning materials on Rhode Island made it an absolute necessity to institute a program of periodic sorties into enemy-held territory to gather up needed supplies, particularly firewood. One detail of 100 men in seven or eight transports sailed for Long Island toward the end of August 1777 on such a mission. Interestingly, several inhabitants of Newport were allowed to join the convoy in smaller boats to collect and bring back firewood for their own use.

A subsequent "wood detail" headed for Shelter Island in mid-October despite a less than satisfactory return at an earlier collection effort. This time, one of the British regiments was ordered to embark on a special mission, first following the others out of the bay and then splitting off to conduct a raid on New Bedford. In the days prior to their departure, reports of the Americans collecting many boats in Providence for a planned attack on the island became more persistent. Information that enemy troops were being assembled near Howland's Ferry and that several hundred boats had been moved to the Kickemuit River from Providence, prompted the raid on New Bedford to be canceled.

In light of this threat, all troops were instructed to clean and maintain their arms in good order while each man was issued sixty rounds and flints. These actions, viewed as a whole, can be interpreted as calling for a heightened state of preparedness.

The islands in the lower bay area, including several small towns along the shore, had been the object of periodic incursions and raids by British troops even before the December 1776 en-masse landings in Newport. So was the case of Prudence Island, where Captain Wallace's patrolling fleet put some 250 soldiers ashore on January 12, 1776. The soldiers burned seven dwellings, seized some sheep and dispersed a group of Minutemen during this raid. The following day a group of Americans from Warren and other nearby settlements reportedly came to the island in whaleboats and engaged the British in an action lasting three hours, during which the British lost fourteen men. The Warren party suffered four dead and one man lost due to capture.

In Wickford, the port village of North Kingstown, a company of Newton's Rangers was captured by the British at Poplar Point. Sometime later in 1777, a bargeload of British soldiers came ashore with intentions of burning the village of Wickford. Unknown to the invaders, a cannon from South Kingstown had been moved into the area where it was positioned at the point. Firing at the landing party from there, the Americans killed one raider. The remaining British raiders—said to have totaled 119 soldiers—retreated to their ship.

On August 3, 1777, a rebel gun battery situated along the Narragansett shoreline fired on the British warship *Renown*, requiring the ship to move farther up the bay. The following day, a detail of some 200 British soldiers made an incursion onto the rebel-held shore of South Kingstown to silence the guns that had fired on the *Renown*. They spiked the only cannon they found. A few skirmishes ensued before the raiding party withdrew with four rebel prisoners.

A combined British-Hessian detail of 100 men embarked on November 5 to visit Shelter Island for another supply of firewood. As usual, the convoy consisting of several transports, was being escorted by a frigate. As the ships headed south toward the open sea, the frigate and a transport ran aground at Point Judith. Onshore militia took advantage of the situation by moving up a cannon and successfully placing the frigate under fire. The captain was forced to surrender ship and crew. A relief party arrived at the scene soon after and was able to save the troops onboard the transport. Several days later, when it was realized that the frigate could not be saved or salvaged, a British detail torched the ship. Ten days later, the sixty seamen who had been captured were returned to Newport and exchanged under a flag of truce.

Raids and Incursions

Several weeks earlier, on October 15, a British ship sailed to Providence under a flag of truce and was detained there when one of the officers was observed sketching a map of the harbor and the ships at anchor. Two weeks later this ship was allowed to return to Newport. MacKenzie assumes it had been held the extra time because any activities the British crew may have observed while in the harbor of Providence could possibly have been used to the detriment of ongoing American staging operations in the area of Howland's Ferry. This attempt to deny the British information notwithstanding, reports were being received during that same period indicating that many of the patriots were leaving their units and returning to their homes. In such case an attack on the island appeared less than probable for the moment. In line with the reduced threat of an impending attack, but also for reasons of safety, all nonessential guns that had been stored at the Artillery Park were moved to Newport during the first days of November.

Local Rotations

During late 1777, the Hessian von Ditfurth and Landgrave Regiments were encamped to the west of Windmill Hill (Butts Hill), with the British 43rd to the rear of the hill. The British 54th Regiment was stationed on Quaker Hill and the two flanking companies at Fogland Ferry. The two Hessian chasseur companies were located approximately one mile south of Fogland Ferry and the British 22nd Regiment was assigned to a site identified by MacKenzie as "Lopez's house." The Hessian von Huyn and von Bünau Regiments were holding positions on the high ground above Easton's Beach. Also, a detail of 100 men of the British 54th was at that time working on earthworks near the town. This group was encamped near three windmills for the duration. A detail of sixty men also occupied Conanicut Island.

The disposition of troops on Rhode Island was never static, however there were constant movements of units based upon the latest available information regarding the enemy. During the early days of December 1777, a planned rotation of troops got underway in anticipation of the approaching colder winter weather. For instance, the Hessian chasseurs moved into winter quarters in the town of Newport while the von Ditfurth Regiment left its encampment area and marched to a barracks site at the island's north end.

Most all of the remaining British and Hessian units were also moved into Newport. Essentially, only one regiment was being maintained in the field along with a limited number of artillery personnel, sufficient to guard and observe enemy movements on the Tiverton and Bristol shores. During the winter months troops were rotated between the field positions on the north end and their winter quarters in the town on a monthly basis. With the increased number of troops housed within Newport, the routine garrison duties were alternated among Hessian and British troops. Due to the concentration of so large a number of personnel in the town, i.e. at the southern end of Rhode Island, troops were alerted to maintain their equipment in good order and to be prepared to move out at moment's notice.

Despite preparing for most of his men to winter-over in the town, General Pigot was concerned about the possibility of an enemy attempt to occupy Conanicut Island with a force coming from the mainland to the east, which could endanger future passage to and from the Bay. To forestall such possibility a British detail of fifty men plus officers and a small cannon with gun crew were assigned to Conanicut on December 9, where they established themselves in a redoubt that had been worked on during the summer. The British engineer proposed another redoubt be built on the high ground overlooking the beach and the approaches to Beavertail as an additional means of controlling any possible enemy advance across the island toward the Dumplings. Two days later, another detail of fifty troops departed for Conanicut to cut wood for the Newport garrison. Each night this group returned to their transport which was at anchor near the ferry landing, to sleep.

There was great joy among the troops, the Hessians in particular, when a group of supply ships arrived from New York on December 15, for their cargo included much-needed clothing as well as camping and tentage equipment for the Hessian regiments. A month prior to the arrival of this convoy, many of the Hessians' tents had been knocked down and torn to shreds during an exceptionally fierce rainstorm. The loss of these field-type shelters was attributed to the age of the tents, which had not been replaced since first issued in Germany. A similar situation existed with regard to the Hessians' uniforms. Many had been torn and patched as a result of

RAIDS AND INCURSIONS

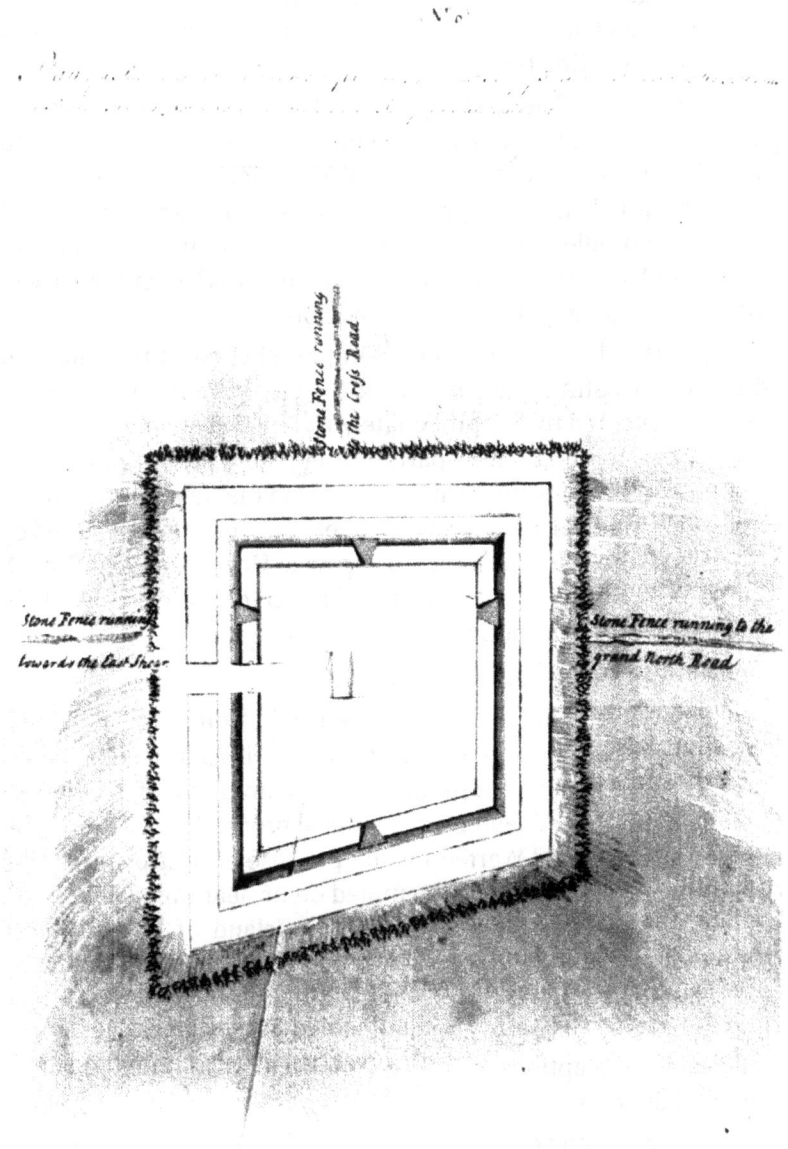

Plan of redoubt erected near the crossroads on Conanicut Island.
Clements Library, University of Michigan, Ann Arbor, MI

earlier engagements in the New York area, and until this time replacements had not been made available to any of the troops in Newport, including the British.

It was not until mid-March, 1778, however, that the Hessians were allowed to put on their new uniforms. It is said permission to do so had been delayed by General Knyphausen. No reason for the three-month delay was given. One might surmise that General Knyphausen held back on the order to change into the new uniforms until after the winter thaw when there was less of a chance of immediately soiling the new issue of clothing.

Ships visited Newport in increasing numbers over the course of time, culminating toward the end of December 1777, when MacKenzie noted that approximately 100 were at anchor in the bay, the most ever seen in these parts. Among these was a sizable number of two-decked former ships-of-the-line that had been converted to haul supplies, plus several frigates. This influx was inspired by reports on the rebel presence at or near Howland's Ferry which spoke of an increase in the number of troops observed although no unusual activity was noticeable.

THE BRISTOL-WARREN AND FALL RIVER RAIDS

The largest raid on enemy-held territory from New England's Newport Base was made on May 24 and 25, 1778 by a detail of 500 British and Hessian troops under the command of Lieutenant Colonel Campbell. Their objective was to proceed to the Kickemuit River via Bristol and Warren for the purpose of destroying a large quantity of flatboats being assembled on or near the river, thereby foiling the enemy's plans to attack the island of Rhode Island. Although various sources have reported on this operation, a Hessian report of June 11, 1778 appearing in the August 1 issue of the *Bayreuther Zeitungen* is cited here in abbreviated form since it reflects the perceptions and observations of Hessians who participated in the raid:

> On the evening of May 24, Lieutenant Colonel Campbell marched to Arnolds Point with part of the 22nd Regiment, flankers of the 54th, and the Hessian chasseurs under Captain Noltenius from Newport. At midnight the 500 men embarked on flatboats under the direction of Sea Captain Clayton and

RAIDS AND INCURSIONS

Plan of attack for the May 25, 1778, raid on Bristol and Warren.
Clements Library, University of Michigan, Ann Arbor, MI

Lieutenant Knowles and headed for Warren River where they landed one mile above Bristol and three miles south of Warren, while the Royal ship *Flora* was patrolling off Papasquash Point. Campbell detailed Captain Seir to demolish a rebel eighteen-pounder at Papasquash Point where an

The raid on Bristol and Warren. *Commonwealth Land Title Insurance Company, 1926*

artillery captain and seven men were captured.

Early the next morning the main element proceeded to Warren and the Kickamuit River where they came upon the enemy boats. Stacked in piles, 125 were burned, some fifty feet long. A gallery of six twelve-pounders and two loaded sloops, a mill, and a bridge across the river were set on fire. The cannons from the gallery plus three eighteen-pounders were spiked and their carriages burned.

After the raid the troops returned to Warren where the chasseurs had spiked two twenty-four pounders, two eighteen-pounders and two nine-pounders that had been left in an artillery park. A new private sloop in the Warren River, the Town Hall, the Baptist Church and several houses were also burned to the ground. Mission accomplished, the troops returned to Bristol where a magazine, the Episcopal Church and several houses were set on fire as they left the town. The rebels fired on them, but their two eighteen-pounders were taken and spiked.

The entire operation was completed with few casualties. Captured (by the British): One Colonel, two Captains and sixty-eight others, mostly members of the military. Captain Noltenius of the Hessian Chasseurs and Lieutenant Meisheimer, General Lossberg's Field Adjutant, distinguished themselves, as did Sea Captain Clayton, who brought the men back safely in their flatboats during the night.

Another Hessian source states that the Hessians suffered two wounded while British casualties amounted to two wounded and two killed. Colonel William Barton received a disabling wound fighting Colonel Campbell's troops at Bristol Point. Other sources indicate that nineteen buildings were destroyed in Bristol and others looted. In Warren many houses were reportedly pillaged, cattle and poultry killed, and a powder magazine as well as the Baptist Meeting House and parsonages burned.

On May 31, 1778 another expedition was undertaken. Major Eyre and 100 men joined a naval operation that sailed past Bristol Ferry into Mount Hope Bay and from there to Fall River where the troops destroyed a sawmill, a corn mill, several large boats, and several thousand feet of planking used for boat building. During this operation the landing party ran into rebel fire and returned to their ships rather than engage the enemy. While this too was a successful raid into enemy territory, it became costly because one of the British galleys ran aground in the upper part of the bay enroute to the operational area. The convoy continued on to Fall River despite the alarms given by enemy sentries along their shore. On the convoy's return trip, the foot soldiers were landed at the north point of Commonfence Neck to assist in defending and saving the stranded galley. This was ultimately accomplished, but only after considerable bombarding of the enemy's shore batteries, in particular the guns at Bristol Ferry.

CHAPTER 14

The Treaty of Paris

ALL'S QUIET IN NEWPORT

Activities in Newport during the first half of 1778 were much the same as they had been during the prior year, with troops moving periodically about the island to alternative sites. Captain von der Malsburg and his unit of chasseurs were ordered to Windmill Hill and Fogland Ferry during the first days of January to relieve the von Ditfurth Regiment, allowing them to move into winter quarters in Newport. A month later, Captain Noltenius moved to Fogland Ferry with his chasseurs to relieve von der Malsburg's men after they had spent their prescribed thirty days in the field. Several armed raids and the series of incursions into enemy territory to collect firewood for the Newport garrison mentioned earlier neither changed the relative quiet nor altered the heightened alert status under which the troops had been laboring. They had become accustomed to the routine by then.

Social events still ranked high on the calendar during the early days of 1778, with a great ball being held in honor of the Queen of England on January 19. In a letter dated January 31, General von Lossberg reported to his superiors that he had been invited aboard the Admiral's ship along with the English generals to celebrate the occasion of Queen Charlotte's birthday. It was during this time that Colonel von Huyn was promoted to Major General. It is interesting to note an entry in the *Journal of the von Huyn Regiment* for April 1 to the effect that: "womenfolk are beautiful and witty... they have one fault: they side with the rebels." Later, on June 4, the von Bünau Regiment fired a three-volley salute in honor of the King's birthday.

Working to perfect their defenses on Rhode Island, both British

Colonel (later General) Friedrich von Lossberg.
Staatliche Kunstsammlungen Kassel, Germany

and Hessian soldiers engaged in clearing their respective fields of fire and observation in front of the various earthworks and trenches they had been constructing. To do so they knocked down hundreds of buttonwood and locust trees. This tree-clearing occured to the consternation of the citizenry, who often blamed the Hessians. According to MacKenzie, construction of additional redoubts at Tonomy Hill, Irishes, Bannister's, the hospital, and the windmill was commenced on April 18. (It is not clear which windmill MacKenzie may be referring to, however, since several existed on the outskirts of Newport at that time). Regiment von Bünau constructed a redoubt between Howland's Bridge and Commonfence at the end of June.

During the early days of 1778, General von Lossberg wrote a series of letters to his "Esteemed Major General" in which he brought his superiors up-to-date on happenings in Newport and on Rhode Island. He also found opportunities to report some of his general observations and to voice matters that raised his concern. Earlier, in May of 1777, he could not pass up the chance to note, while speaking of the civilian population that: "the gentlemen ride horses during the day and make love at night... blacks do all the work." In his letter of January 6, 1778, he expressed discontent that the Hessians unfurl their regimental flags wherever they went while the British were not required to do so. He was especially concerned about to whom the flag ought to be assigned in the event a regiment were split up. He noted in the same communication that new uniforms had arrived and urged the release of orders allowing the wearing of the new garments. In support of his position he noted that the uniforms being worn were completely torn from wear and dampness. Even some of the newly arrived uniforms got wet and mildewed in transit and needed to be repaired. He reported further that he had inspected some houses on the island that had been readied for torching in the event of an enemy assault. These buildings had been prepared for burning with old rags and sulfur.

In a letter dated March 7, General Lossberg reports having sent ships to New York for supplies, but that they were lost or grounded in a ferocious storm. He also noted that the tents of his troops needed to be replaced, as many were no longer serviceable. The high winds and salty fog being encountered in Newport shortened the life of such equipment. He also pointed out the precarious position of some of the Hessians who had been captured by the enemy (it should be noted that P.O.W.s in the enemy's hands were expected to be supported by their own army), noting that "the prisoners of the rebels need to be supported with funds, and that some prisoners had to use their own money to pay for their support." Lossberg goes on to say that each of the captured Hessians imprisoned by the enemy would be receiving shoes, stockings, a shirt, and 150 guineas in cash. He complained of having had to sign a receipt for the English paymaster in triplicate in return for the pay of his regiments, but having had trouble obtaining a copy.

In a letter dated May 2, 1778, General von Lossberg notes that he was still waiting for the new tents to set up camp, because the old ones were in disrepair and that three-hundred Hessians and many English soldiers were sleeping on the ground each day. At this opportunity he relayed information obtained from spies to the effect that the rebels were concentrating their forces in the north-east, and that General Sullivan was in Providence meeting with a French general. He further noted that the enemy was filling up magazines with ammunition and supplies. Not sure of the enemy's true intent, he wondered if it could all be a bluff.

THE TREATY OF PARIS

Until this time little was known what position the French might take in this conflict, knowing that they had lost vast lands in Canada to the British as a result of the Seven Years' War. Benjamin Franklin had traveled to France in 1776, soon after the Declaration of Independence had been signed, for the purpose of seeking French support in the Revolutionary War. Initially, King Louis XVI was not receptive to French involvement, despite the urging of his foreign minister, the Count Vergennes. After General Burgoyne's surrender to the Americans at Saratoga in October 1777, however, the King agreed to a more formal involvement, having previously only rendered passive help to the American colonists in the form of money and supplies. Benjamin Franklin had successfully waited out the change in French attitude, enabling him to consummate a Treaty of Alliance between France and America on February 6, 1778. Under the treaty the French were able to support the Americans openly with arms, money, and equipment. George Washington's prayers were answered when a French naval squadron sailed for America on April 15, 1778 to assist in subduing the British and Hessian forces that were controlling much of America's eastern coast.

The French fleet sailing from its base in Toulon in the Mediterranean was under the command of Comte Charles Hector d'Estaing. His squadron consisted of twelve capital ships, each armed with from fifty to eighty guns, plus several frigates and smaller boats. He also had some 9,842 seamen and marines at his disposal as well as some 1,500 ground troops that could be landed as may be required. With appropriate changes to ships and personnel there existed possibilities of increasing his landing forces by up to 4,000 men. In July 1778, Comte d'Estaing arrived off the coast of Virginia, sailed up the coast to Sandy Hook, New Jersey, and subsequently headed for Newport at the end of the month.

Admiral Count d'Estaing. Engraving by H.B. Hall's Sons. *Courtesy Glen Cockrum*

MANEUVERS

In early May, General Lossberg moved to the northern end of Rhode Island with 1,000 men from the Landgrave and von Ditfurth Regiments with assigned field pieces. At that time, General von Lossberg was the second in command of the Newport garrison. Regiment von Bünau went into positions at Easton's Redoubt and the von Huyn Regiment took up positions near the windmill south of Newport. Later in the month, four Hessian battalions with eight field pieces were on maneuvers. Lt. MacKenzie noted they made a good appearance. General von Lossberg's letter of May 31, indicated that the artillery participating in the maneuvers was under command of Captain Schleenstein. Coordination among the several units was considered to have been well executed. Target practice using six rounds per man provided by General Pigot was being scheduled for the following week. The von Bünau Regiment moved up to Windmill Hill at the same time. General von Lossberg further noted that the rebels had set up their tents as had the British. Referencing the successful expedition to Bristol and Warren under Colonel Campbell, he praised Captain Noltenius and Lieutenant Roepanack for their leadership of the Hessian contingents.

MORE TROOP MOVEMENTS

On June 11, 1778 Brigadier General Brown arrived from New York with the Provincial Regiment and the Prince of Wales American Volunteers. According to MacKenzie the troop disposition on the island as of June 13, 1778 was as follows: von Bünau stationed at Windmill Hill and all posts at the north end of the island; the 22nd British Regiment at Quaker Hill and at the east shore, the 43rd Regiment to the left of West Road at Turkey Hill and from the left of the von Bünau troops to the creek at Layton Mills. There were eighty Hessians at Fogland Ferry near the 54th British Regiment on East Road at the blacksmith shop. The Landgrave, von Ditfurth, von Huyn Regiments, and the Royal Artillery held positions in Newport. Brown's Volunteers were assigned to the new redoubts near town. Detachments of fifty men spent weekly tours at the redoubt on Conanicut Island. Later in the month. Captain von der Malsburg and two companies of chasseurs were encamped near Elam's farm, between Fogland and Black Point, while the von Huyn Regiment was detailed to the south of town facing Brenton's Neck. It must be noted that the troops were frequently rotated among the many sites comprising the extensive defenses of Newport and vicinity.

ANTICIPATING THE ARRIVAL OF THE FRENCH FLEET

Coming from New York, the captured General Prescott, who had been exchanged for American General Charles Lee, arrived back in Newport on July 15, 1778. He divulged information that the French fleet was heading for the colonies to support the rebels in their struggle against the British-Hessian occupation. This was disturbing news to the troops bottled up in Newport, and some were beginning to wonder what fate might await them in the months ahead. Learning of the simultaneous arrival of reinforcements consisting of some 2,000 men, including two experienced Ansbach-Bayreuth Regiments, the British 38th Regiment of Provincials, and eighty men of the Royal Artillery, brought a sigh of relief at that worrisome moment.

CHAPTER 15

Just in Time—The 1778 Troop Reinforcements

"DIE FRANKEN KOMMEN!"

Hailing from the area of Franconia in southern Germany, the arrival of the combined Ansbach-Bayreuth Regiment was enthusiastically welcomed by the Hessians already serving on Rhode Island. Ansbach-Bayreuth had blood ties to the King of Prussia and the House of Brandenburg through Margrave Alexander, who was a nephew of Frederick the Great. This relationship was carried forward in the letters "M.Z.B." (Markgraf zu Brandenburg) and by the red Brandenburg eagle that appeared on regimental flags.

As ordered by General Clinton "who feared for the weak garrison," the addition of the Franconians to the Newport garrison brought the number of the German-speaking troops in the area back up to their original strength. These reinforcements had first arrived in America on June 3, 1777 after experiencing several rough months at sea. Colonel Friedrich Ludwig Albrecht von Eyb had headed up their march through Germany prior to embarking for America. After his arrival in America he became ill and was hospitalized with fever. Returning to his troops soon after, but wishing he could be at peace so he could spend the rest of his life quietly with his family, the Colonel's request to be relieved was granted and he returned home, taking with him some flying squirrels as a gift for his prince.

When first inspected by General William Howe, the Ansbach-Bayreuth troops were praised for their outstanding state of training and discipline, as well as for the equipment they had brought with them. Some of the men spent much of their time encamped on Staten Island in New York harbor, while others participated in oper-

The uniforms of the Ansbach-Bayreuth regiments.
Courtesy R.J. Marrion and Company of Military Historians

ations aimed at securing the areas north of the city and along the Hudson River. In November 1777, they moved to Philadelphia by ship to participate in the occupation of the city and to winter there. Upon their arrival in America the Franconian Jägers were reassigned to serve with other Hessian Jägers, participating in various campaigns and assignments. Even though the Ansbach-Bayreuth units had not participated in any major battle, they nevertheless suffered close to 100 dead during the year prior to being dispatched to Newport. Most of their casualties resulted from sickness, primarily from typhoid. In addition, the number of desertions among these troops rose steadily during that period, a time when they were becoming increasingly disillusioned and dissatisfied because of short rations and a lack of winter clothing.

In 1778, Rhode Island was experiencing an exceptionally hot summer. The local population was hard-pressed to remember such a heat wave in the past. MacKenzie considered it of sufficient import to make note of it in his diary. Wearing their woolen uniforms at such times must have been true torture for the Hessians and Franconians, and while uniforms were indeed being worn most of the time, there are indications that some liberties were taken occasionally due to the climate encountered in America.

Following their disembarkation in Newport on July 15, the Ansbach-Bayreuth contingent encamped behind the Green End redoubt. A few days later, MacKenzie describes their early deployment as well as his personal disagreement with the strategy and wisdom of that initial assignment:

July 20, 1778   The two Battalions of Ansbach embarked at 9 o'clock in flat boats, and encamped on that part of Conanicut called Beaver's tail. I think this is a most dangerous position. The reason for placing them there is to possess the island and cover the Batteries at Fox Hill (which fires on the Narragansett Passage) and the Dumplins (which fires on the entrance of the harbor). But if the French fleet appears, and succeeds in their attempt to come into the harbor, (which the battery on the Dumplins cannot prevent), we shall inevitably lose those two Battalions; as the withdrawing from Conanicut, after the Enemy has forced an entrance, will be impracticable. We should not therefore risk the loss of so material a part of our force. It would be much preferable to sacrifice a small detachment, sufficient for working the guns and the defense of the Batteries.

(Note: The two Ansbach Regiments entered camp on Conanicut Island under command of Colonel Friedrich August Valentin Voit von Salzburg).

Col. Voit von Salzburg, Commander of Ansbach Regiment.
Bayerisches Armeemuseum, Ingolstadt, Germany

July 21   ...We are completing the Batteries on Brenton's Point, Goat Island, The Dumplins, and Fox Hill...

July 27   ...The Batteries as Brenton's Point, The Dumplins, Fox Hill, Goat Island, and the North Battery, have been mounted with cannon, etc. in the best manner the time will permit.

ENEMY FLEET ON THE HORIZON

Lieutenant Johann Franz Prechtel of the Ansbach Regiment made the following notes in his own diary for the same period:

July 20, 1778   On Monday both Regiments were put across to Conanicut Island from Newport where they went into camp. The water is 3/4 hours wide here. Encamped on Conanicut Island from the 21st to the 28th.

July 29, 1778   At about 11:00 o'clock the French fleet appeared near the Conanicut Island lighthouse and dropped anchor. Our corps recognized them immediately from their white flags. We moved out immediately to advance forward several hundred steps. As we were so doing we received orders to fall back and leave all of our baggage and tents behind. We embarked on flat boats and were taken back to Newport.

MacKenzie's notes for July 29th include the following pertinent comments:

> Boats were immediately sent over to Conanicut, from whence the two battalions of Ansbach and Brown's Regiment of Provincials were withdrawn, leaving small detachments only in the Batteries on Fox Hill and The Dumplins. The withdrawing of these Battalions immediately, was certainly well judged. From the moment the French attempted to enter the harbor, it would have been impracticable, and loss of so considerable a part of our force would have proved disgraceful and perhaps fatal. They should not have been there.

From the tone of MacKenzie's notes regarding the deployment of the large troop contingents to Conanicut Island at a time when the French fleet could to be expected to appear momentarily, one can detect irritation with his superiors' orders. And while he may not have been in command, nor perhaps had he been consulted, he was an officer with years of service and considerable experience that enabled him to develop a strategy of his own although he

Lieutenant Prechtel tells of crossing over to Conanicut Island on July 20, 1778, a distance of three-quarters of an hour by water and sighting the French fleet on July 29. *The Huntington Library, San Marino, CA*

lacked the power of implementation. His disgust is reinforced by suspension of overall operations of the army until it was known more specifically what the French fleet was preparing to do. In this regard, he stated in his diary notes of July 26:

So extraordinary an event as the present, certainly never

before occurred in the history of Britain! An army of 50,000 men, and a fleet of near 100 ships and armed vessels, are prevented from acting offensively by the appearance on the American coast of a French Squadron of twelve sail of the line and four frigates, without troops. Some unpardonable faults have been committed somewhere; and those whose duty it is to watch the motions of the enemy in every quarter, should answer with their heads for risking the fate of so large a portion of the national force...

While much attention was being focused on Conanicut Island and the French fleet assembled at the entrances to Narragansett Bay, many last-minute actions were being taken in Newport in an effort to be better prepared to receive and engage the French when they ventured into the bay. British frigates were ordered to stay close to the shoreline and land their guns, stores, and provisions as soon as it was certain that the approaching fleet was French. Some hasty troop movements were simultaneously initiated in the Newport area where the 54th British regiment was pulled back to complete the defensive works at the North Battery. Concurrently, all available carts were collected to move stores, provisions, and ammunition from the lower part of town to more protected areas. As part of this realignment, the Bayreuth troops moved to Tonomy Hill to occupy the fort at that strategic location.

At daybreak on July 30th, the French sent one of their ships into the Bay via the West Passage. MacKenzie reported this incident as follows:

At 6:00 a.m. she reached opposite Fox Hill battery, which fired four twenty-four-pound shot at her, each of which she returned with seven or eight. However, she passed without any apparent damage, and at about 7 o'clock anchored halfway between the north point of Conanicut and Hope Islands.

In the meantime, another large French ship drew closer to the southern point of Brenton's Neck, where it anchored along with two additional ships from the fleet, while two French frigates were observed entering the Sakonnet River.

Under the given circumstances there was little to be gained by attempting to defend Conanicut Island actively. The final disposition of the matter is described by MacKenzie when he wrote:

> The General, judging it would answer but little purpose to risk the loss of the Detachments upon Conanicut, sent orders, as soon as the French ship had passed the Battery on Fox Hill, to withdraw them and the guns from the island. The troops were brought off; but as there was not a sufficient number of oxen to remove the guns, those on Fox Hill were spiked, and the two twenty-four-pounders on the Dumplins were thrown down the rock into the sea. The island was entirely evacuated by 10 o'clock, without any interruption.

The *Journal of Regiment von Huyn* noted that the powder magazine on Conanicut had been set on fire before the last troop contingent departed. Captain von der Malsburg notes in his diary for July 30:

> We heard brisk cannonading; the reason for this was that two French ships of seventy-four guns had passed our battery at Beavertail at the southern end of Conanicut Island in order to shut us in more closely, and had penetrated into Narragansett passage... As there was nothing now to prevent the enemy from taking possession of Conanicut Island, this soon took place after the aforementioned battery had been abandoned by our soldiers, the guns spiked and the powder magazine blown up.

With the French fleet under Comte d'Estaing at their door poised for an attack and the entrances to the Bay blocked by the hostile armada, "the British authorities were at their wit's end," the *Journal of Regiment von Huyn* noted.

> No one could advise them. However lively it was in all the streets, it looked very disorderly and desolate everywhere. The tradespeople closed their shops and each one endeavored to stow away and secure his possessions as well as and as safely as they could. The three batteries commanding the harbor were strengthened and supplied with several guns and everything placed in proper condition for defense. Our men had to work incessantly and dare not undress at night. Although we had a three-month's stock of provisions in hand, our Commander-in-Chief took the precaution, in case we should only be blockaded, to collect all the cattle on the island and

drive them into the dunes, leaving one behind, however, for each owner.

From the prison ship in the harbor, a total of seventy-four rebel prisoners were brought ashore and initially handed over to Captain von der Malsburg for his men to guard. At that time, the ongoing shifting of troops had left his left flank unprotected, nor was there any longer reliable naval protection available. He appealed to General Pigot to move the prisoners into vacant barracks within the redoubt at Fogland Ferry for confinement. This request was approved, and von der Malsburg was once again able to carry out his assigned chasseur duties.

MacKenzie continues his diary for July 30, 1778, saying:

> The French took possession of Conanicut this day and hoisted their white colors there. It is expected the rebels will place some guns in the battery on the Dumplins in order to annoy our battery on Brenton's point and facilitate entry of the French fleet... It is the General's intention to withdraw the troops from the outposts on the island and concentrate his whole force for the defense of the positions near the town, as soon as the French fleet enters the harbor.

He continues on July 31st with the following interesting words:

> It has been determined this morning by the generals to withdraw the troops from the north part of the Island, bring off all cannon and stores, burn all the barracks, and drive in all the cattle and horses, as soon as it becomes evident that the French fleet are determined to force an entrance into the harbor. Everything is to be withdrawn within the new redoubts, and our defense on the island side is to be confined to that height and position from Tonomy Hill on the left, round by Green End and Easton's beach on the right.

CHAPTER 16

The 1778 Siege of Newport

General Washington felt a combined attack of American and French forces on Newport could result in the capture of the entire British garrison of some 6,000 men. It was thus agreed with French Vice Admiral Count d'Estaing that a joint operation would get underway in early summer 1778. Major General John Sullivan commanded an army of approximately 11,000 Americans which he assembled in Tiverton across the waters of the Sakonnet River at the northern end of Rhode Island.

A TIME OF UNCERTAINTY

With several French ships passing into the bay via the western passage and the bulk of the fleet poised to follow, the British withdrew their troops and cannon from Windmill Hill (Butts Hill) as well as other outlying sites, to take up and arm positions prepared earlier for the defense of Newport.

Tempers were running high—as might be expected—and enemy collaborators were among the defender's immediate targets. Captain von der Malsburg reported that a man had been arrested on August 1 while signaling the hostile vessels, and that his men were getting ready to meet any French landing party on the beach at the point of their bayonets. Newport became a closed town by August 6, with only personnel of the occupation forces allowed on the streets. The von Ditfurth Regiment moved 200 of its troops to Tonomy Hill to man the cannons at that site, while the British 22nd, 43rd, Brown's, and Fanning's Regiments, plus the First Ansbach, von Huyn, and Landgrave Regiments occupied the first line of defenses with their left flank anchored at Tonomy Hill. A second line even closer to town extended along what Lieutenant

The French Squadron Entering Newport under Fire from the Batteries and Forcing a Passage, August 8, 1778, as shown in this wash drawing by Pierre Ozanne. *Library of Congress*

MacKenzie identified by way of key points that included Easton's House, the Library, Brindley's Rope House, a Windmill, Barrier's Redoubt, and Durfee's House. These, together with the harbor area, were occupied by the British 38th and 54th Regiments, the Second Ansbach, the von Ditfurth and von Bünau Regiments, and the chasseur units.

On August 5, the British ran their Frigate *Cerberus* aground and set it on fire to avoid two French ships that had been anchored at the north end of Conanicut Island. Soon after the *Juno*, lying near Coddington Cove, was also set on fire. Both crews reached shore safely before their ships blew up. Observing additional French sail approaching between Prudence and Rhode Island, the *Orpheus*, *Lark*, and *Pigot* were likewise run on shore and set afire. Their crews were also saved before the ships exploded. The *Lark* had been run aground farthest north at Freeborn's Creek, where burning debris from her explosion was observed as far inland as the Windmill Hill redoubt. A nearby dwelling was at the same time consumed by flames after being hit by flying tinder. During the night four French battle ships joined others already in the bay off Newport. Several small privateers were sighted on the bay at the same time, with

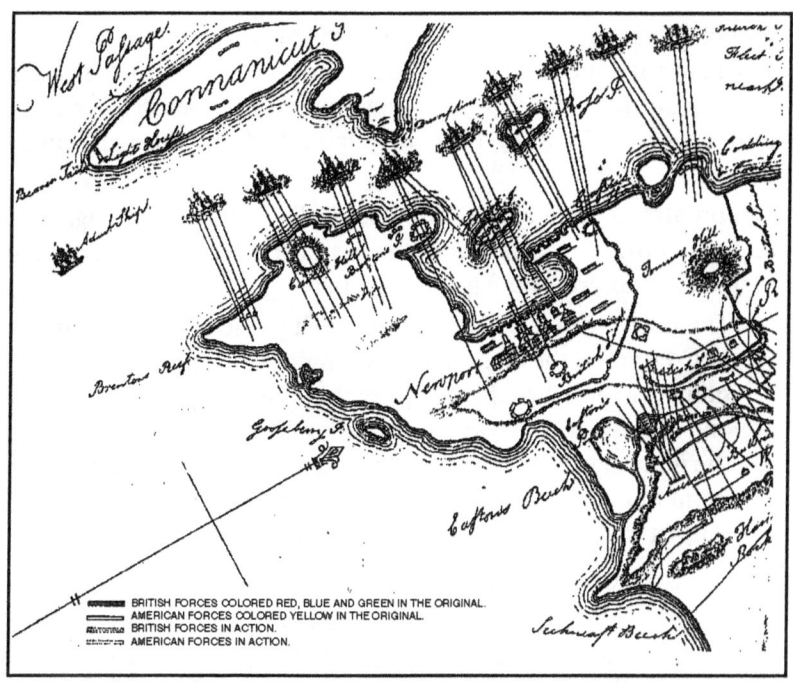

Section of map showing French fleet entering Newport harbor.
Harvard University, Cambridge, MA

MacKenzie reporting the landing of a rebel officer and twenty men who plundered the Stoddard and Potter houses, beating and ill-treating the women.

The *Journal of Regiment von Ditfurth* noted on August 8 that the French ships were being fired upon by the batteries at Brenton's Neck, Kings Battery at Goat Island, and the North Battery, and that the ships responded in kind, with some of their cannon balls hitting the town. The land-borne soldiers of the Newport garrison took cover as much as their situation would permit. After moving past the batteries and into the bay, the ships anchored off Conanicut Island. The dueling of the guns on both sides is said to have lasted more than one hour.

According to von der Malsburg, several houses in the line of fire of some of the fortified positions were burned down by loyal Rhode Islanders. Houses near Bannisters' Hill experienced the same fate. In addition to the named ships, the British sank several large transports close to shore in the vicinity of North Battery to prevent a

French advance in that vicinity. British ships' crews that had been forced ashore due to the loss of their hulls were assigned to defensive positions on land, where they manned the available guns—duties with which they were very familiar from their shipboard details.

Soon after a large ship of the East India Company ran aground and was burned within twenty yards of the wharves. Lieutenant MacKenzie describes the state of panic:

> The burning of the houses and the ship, the sinking of our only Frigates, the sight of the enemy's fleet within the harbour, the retreat of the troops within the lines, and the dismay and distress so strongly impressed upon the countenances of the inhabitants, who concluded that the rebels were on the point of landing, and their lives and property were in the utmost danger, formed together a very extraordinary scene.

GENERAL SULLIVAN MOVES ON NEWPORT

Early on the morning of August 9th, General Sullivan, coming from Tiverton, landed an initial contingent of troops at Howland's Ferry in eighty-six flatboats. He promptly advanced to the Butts Hill fortifications that had been abandoned by the British when they retreated to their defensive lines on Newport's outskirts. Sullivan next gave orders to march on Newport. French Admiral d'Estaing considered Sullivan's move premature in that the attack on Newport was to have been a joint ground operation between the 4,000 troops he had landed on Conanicut Island and Sullivan's army of 11,000. While Sullivan had seized the opportunity to occupy the north end of Rhode Island immediately following the British evacuation, his move appeared to have preempted or at least taken some punch out of d'Estaing's own plans. An aristocrat, d'Estaing was not prone to taking orders under any circumstances from Sullivan, a commoner. Sullivan's vanguards advanced to Peckham's, Redwood's and Honeyman's Hill on their march to Newport. Waiting for the French to make any supporting movements, Sullivan's men held positions at Honeyman's Hill and Green End.

About that same time, a British fleet of thirty-six vessels (as observed from Tonomy Hill) appeared on the horizon off Newport. This fleet, under Admiral Richard Howe, had sailed from New York

General John Sullivan, commander of American forces in the Battle of Rhode Island. *Line of Battle, Naval Heritage Museum, Canton, GA*

with reinforcements received when Admiral Byron's fleet arrived from England. While the beleaguered troops in Newport had given up any hope of receiving help in time to thwart a possible coordinated attack by American and French ground forces, the appearance of the fleet had an encouraging effect on garrison personnel. While that in itself was good news, d'Estaing's action to leave the bay and meet his enemy farther out at sea made the situation even better for the troops under siege.

FRENCH FLEET DEPARTS

There was much activity aboard the French ships in Narragansett Bay on the days following the sighting of Admiral Howe's approaching fleet. French troops quickly evacuated Conanicut Island and reboarded their respective ships on August 9 and 10, 1778. A hospital that had been set up there was also packed up and moved out. Soon the French fleet raised their anchors and headed for the open sea to escape being bottled up inside the bay, and to engage Admiral Howe's ships. As d'Estaing's fleet exited the bay, endless gunfire came from both sides.

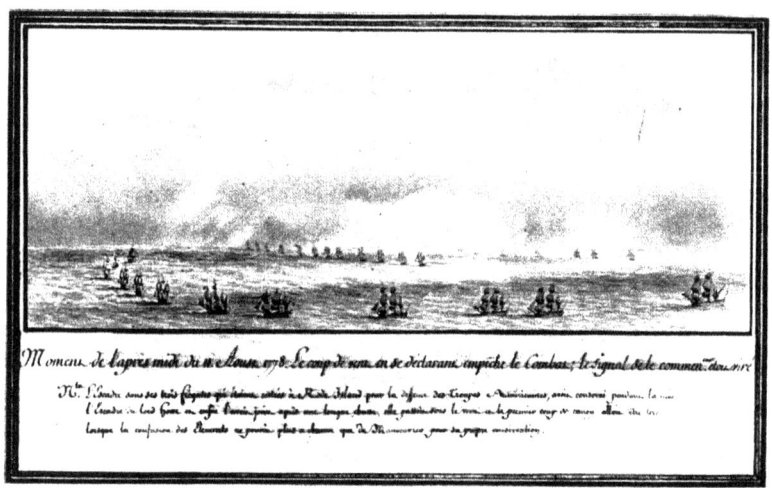

French Fleet leaves Narragansett Bay to engage the British fleet under Admiral Howe. Wash drawing by Pierre Ozanne. *Library of Congress*

Fort George on Goat Island and the guns at Brenton's Point were extensively involved in the exchange of cannon fire. These positions were favorably located to inflict damage on d'Estaing's departing ships. The long-range dueling produced a number of casualties among the French, who threw their dead overboard. The floating bodies were witnessed by the British and Hessian defenders who at that time were confined to a small bridgehead that encircled the town of Newport.

Lieutenant MacKenzie estimates that no less than 2,500 cannon shot were fired during that maneuver. Many French cannon balls fell inside the town, but the damage was reported as minimal. The bombardment was nevertheless so heavy that the besieged troops offered many prayers for their well-being and took cover and hugged the ground in their redoubts and trenches. It was noted that one forty-eight-pound shot fell 200 yards beyond the library, which sits on the highest ground above the town. Captain von der Malsburg commented that enemy cannon fire not only pierced the ramparts, but flew with greater force than expected.

Land-based observers watched as the French fleet approached Admiral Howe's ships. Soon the ships of both fleets disappeared beyond the horizon. Both Captain von der Malsburg and Lieutenant MacKenzie reported that a severe storm hit Newport on August 12 and 13. Many tents were blown down, and von der Malsburg was forced to seek shelter at a coach house near his position. Arms and gunpowder were simultaneously rendered useless because of the heavy rain. It was during this storm that the two fleets, farther out at sea by then, received excessive battering by the elements, resulting in considerable damage to both. Nevertheless, General Sullivan's men continued perfecting their positions along the perimeter of the encircled British and Hessian garrison of Newport by constructing additional positions and bringing in more cannon. They kept up their harassing fire, forcing the besieged to be cautious in their movements, or be subjected to deadly cannon fire. Sullivan held on to these positions for more than ten days, establishing his own headquarters on Honeyman Hill.

Finally, on August 20, the French fleet reappeared. On sighting the approaching ships, the Americans, who had a strangling hold on Newport, hoped for that long-awaited joint push to dislodge the besieged garrison. Instead, d'Estaing elected to sail for Boston to repair and refit the ships of his fleet, many of which had been demasted and seriously battered during the recent storm at sea.

Siege Flounders

Understandably, General Sullivan was furious at the sudden departure of the French fleet, feeling he had been left stranded by d'Estaing. His hopes of taking Newport were shattered, not only by the departure of the French, but also because of the departure of large numbers of his own troops, some of whom had enlisted for very short periods of service. MacKenzie was aware that some of

Sullivan's militia had enlisted for only twenty days, and that they could be expected to go home after that time. The significant loss of this temporary manpower at such a critical time was detrimental to Sullivan's more ambitious plans to storm Newport with the help of French troops to force the surrender of the British and their Hessian allies. General Lafayette, a French nobleman who was with Sullivan at the time, rode to Boston to meet with d'Estaing in hopes of expediting the repairs to his ships and the return of the fleet to Narragansett Bay, or as an alternative, for the French troops to march from Boston on foot to come to Sullivan's aid. Regrettably, his mission ended without success because of the timing of Sullivan's evacuation.

According to MacKenzie, after the French had cleared the bay, British scouting parties once again ventured across the water to Conanicut Island. On one of these missions, carried out on August 22nd, a detail from the 22nd Regiment brought a man by the name of Eldridge back from the island who provided information regarding rebel intentions. He is quoted as having said that d'Estaing would not return to the area on the assumption that British Admiral Howe's fleet might still be in the vicinity. Reliable or not, this was the kind of information the besieged troops wanted very much to believe.

On August 27, three British support ships arrived, in itself good reason for jubilation in the beleaguered garrison. News that General Charles Grey had arrived in New York with 3,500 men who were to be sent to Newport to relieve the besieged city brought even greater hopes and joy. On the American side a council of war decided that Sullivan's army should fall back and return to the north end of Rhode Island.

At that time, the British order of battle had Major General Prescott commanding the second line of defenses (those closest to Newport), Brigadier General Smith the right wing (eastern side), and Hessian General von Lossberg the left wing (western side) of the first line, or outer line of defenses.

CHAPTER 17

Battle of Rhode Island

Left in the lurch by the unexpected withdrawal of the French fleet, Major General John Sullivan ordered his troops, at that time entrenched along the perimeter of the heavily defended town of Newport, to withdraw to the northern end of the island. When Lieutenant MacKenzie at daybreak on August 29 observed that the enemy had struck their tents, he relayed the information to General Pigot as quickly as possible. In his capacity of British brigade major, MacKenzie ordered Captain von der Malsburg and his Hessian chasseurs to march to Irish's Redoubt without delay, where they would receive further instructions.

PIGOT SEIZES INITIATIVE

Acting on this information, General Pigot ordered the pursuit of the withdrawing enemy by 2,000 men consisting of light infantry, grenadiers, the Ansbach-Bayreuth regiments, and some field pieces. Major General von Lossberg was in overall command of the Hessian column whose operational area embraced the left flank of the British-Hessian advance. More specifically, von der Malsburg was to cautiously advance northward along West Road with an advance detail of 147 men, attacking Sullivan's rear guard wherever possible and harassing the enemy at every opportunity.

Simultaneously, the British 38th and 54th Regiments under Major General Prescott pursued the retreating Americans along the right flank, or East Road, in an effort to engage them in that area. Brigadier Smith proceeded toward Quaker Hill, keeping to the section between East and West Roads. His formation consisted of the flanking companies of the 38th and 54th, plus the 22nd and 43rd Regiments.

The Hessian chasseurs moved out quickly. By 7:00 a.m. they were some three miles ahead of their own main body, advancing under the sound of their drums and fifes, and without encountering any resistance. About that time Captain von der Malsburg spotted some entrenchments on Redwood's Hill that were occupied by enemy personnel. It appears that Colonel John Laurens, son of the president of the Continental Congress, was dug in at that site with the rear guard of Sullivan's army. The chasseurs surrounded the high ground, and shouting "Huzza-huzza" charged uphill, storming the position with fixed bayonets.

The *Journal of Captain Friedrich von der Malsburg* provides further details that are synopsized here:

> The Americans abandoned the position and fell back to another height that was occupied by troops in blue and white. This work was also taken by storm. The Hessians lost some dead and wounded. Captain Noltinius (commander of the second chasseur company) was wounded. The Americans drew back.

Captain von der Malsburg recorded that he received a slight wound to his hand during this early engagement. Although some of the enemy wounded were asking for water, their pleas fell on deaf ears for the most part. The Hessians, who were wearing their uncomfortably hot woolen uniforms on this exceptionally exhausting day, had little or none to spare.

BRITISH COLUMN AMBUSHED

Not far to the east, Colonel Henry Beekman Livingston was in command of troops deployed near the intersection of Union Street and East Road. A deadly skirmish developed when Colonel Campbell's 22nd Regiment ran into Livingston's ambush near the intersection, resulting in many dead and wounded that fell victim to the hail of enemy musket fire coming from behind nearby stone walls. The battle sounds of this fierce encounter was heard by the Hessians at the western end of Union Street who dispatched a large detail "on-the-double" to assist the British at the far end of the road. They arrived too late to be of any help. The Americans had quickly withdrawn following their successful surprise ambush of the British lead column.

Mrs. Mary Almy, wife of Benjamin Almy, vividly described her observations and impressions of the bloody engagement that took place in the vicinity of their residence on Rhode Island. Her remembrances are recounted here in abbreviated form only, yet her recollection of the events of the day are sufficiently illustrative to provide the reader with a realistic description of the ground actions that took place during the early hours of what has become known as the Battle of Rhode Island. She noted in part:

> The Hessians overtook a party on the West Road near the Redwood barn; they pursued with violence while the others retreated with prudence leaving the roads strewn with dead bodies. The East Road was a scene of blood and slaughter from Cousin Almy's down to the foot of Quaker Hill.... Provincials halted at Windmill Hill and were followed by the King's troops when a smart battle ensued. The 22nd, 43rd, Ansbach and von Huyn troops met with great loss. The wounded were hauled away in carts, all available carts being engaged for this purpose.

Starting about 9 o'clock in the morning a cannonade got underway involving the guns on both sides which lasted most of the day. Stephen Popp, one of the Ansbach-Bayreuth troops who observed the long-range duel between the enemy's guns and their own, felt that the cannon fire was ineffective until grapeshot was used. In their continuing northward push the Hessians were able to exert sufficient pressure on Sullivan's line to force his withdrawal to the artillery redoubt and Windmill Hill (Butts Hill). In so doing, the rebel forces established their own new line of defenses, on an east-west axis across the island.

THE BATTLE UNFOLDS

The American order of battle placed the units available to Major General Sullivan in the hands of the following commanders, listed from east to west across the northern end of Rhode Island: Tyler, Glover, Greene, Cornell, Varnum, and Livingston. Apparently the swiftness with which the Hessians initially advanced had not been anticipated. It is rumored that General Greene was eating in a nearby farmhouse when he saw the Hessian chasseurs swarming up the slopes of the hill he was to defend, and that only the swiftness of his horse saved him from being captured.

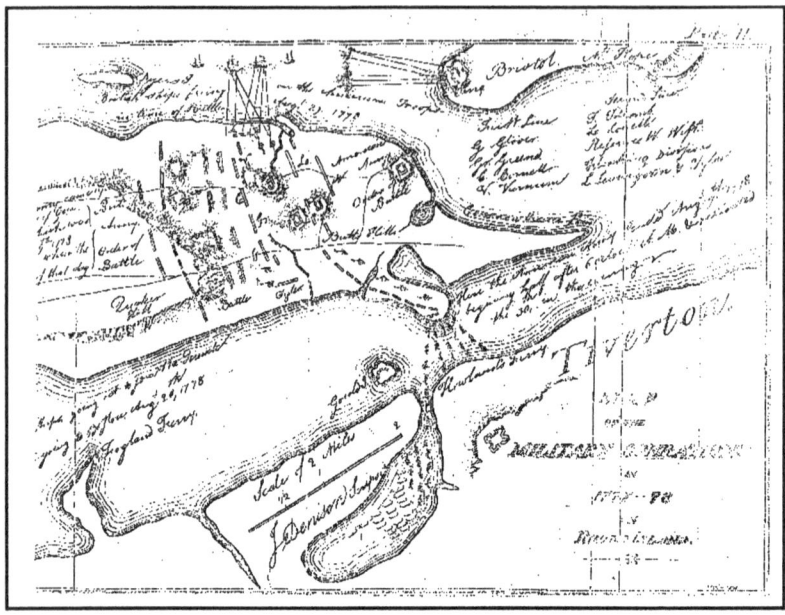

Section of map showing the operations under the command of Major General Sullivan. *Harvard University, Cambridge, MA*

Lieutenant MacKenzie observed that the weight of the action to drive the rebels from Quaker Hill fell on the flank companies and the 22nd Regiment. Captain von der Malsburg and his chasseurs had been hot on the heels of Sullivan's retiring forces, as were the other Hessian and Ansbach-Bayreuth troops that had been committed to the operations on West Road. One of von der Malsburg's wounded men cautioned him that the enemy was laying in ambush at their right flank. The chasseurs charged and dislodged the enemy quickly. Next came the run for Turkey Hill, from which the enemy had to be dislodged. During this phase of the operation the von Huyn and Fanning Regiments drove the enemy out of the swamp on the north side of Turkey Hill. From there, it was onward toward rebel-held Barrington's Hill, a redoubt that was presently being armed with three guns that were able to open fire in time to impact the Hessian advance.

Resistance on the American side got tougher, impairing the Hessian charge. A shortage of ammunition proved another serious obstacle that prevented any quick victory for the British. The slow-

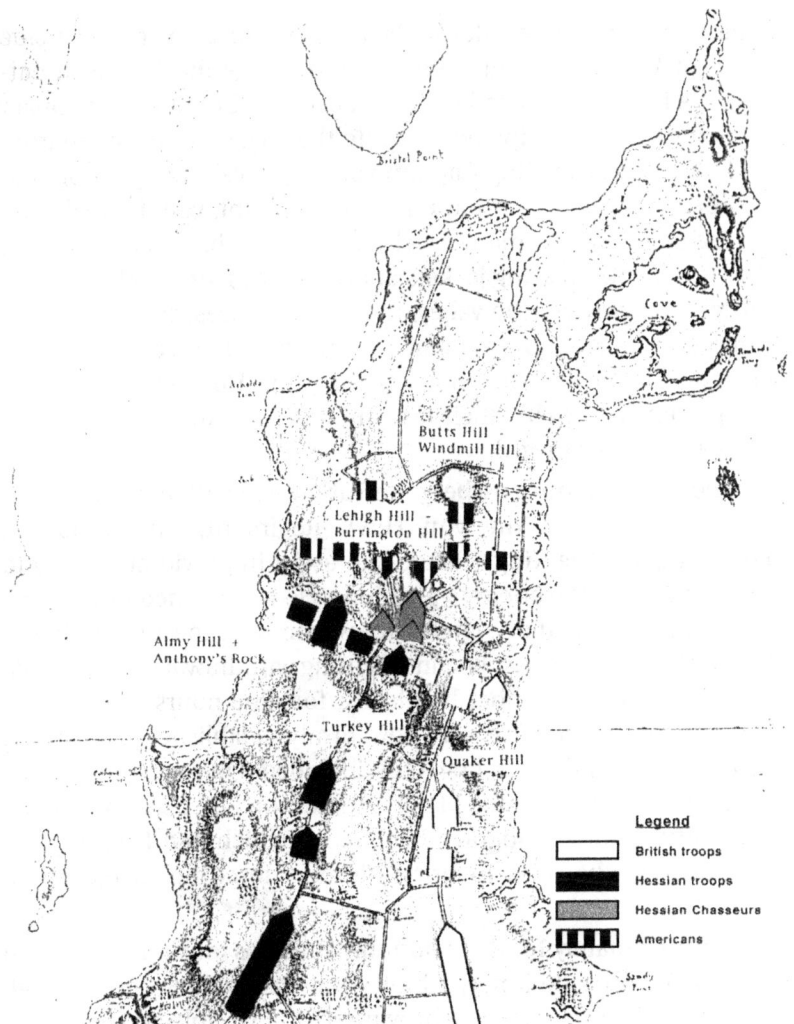

The Battle of Rhode Island. *Author's sketch*

down of the Hessians benefitted the defenders, who took advantage of the situation by creeping to within close range of their opponents' positions to harass them with musket fire. During this precarious time, Captain von der Malsburg and his men were pinned down, forced to take advantage of nearby stone walls for cover, and bide their time until a new supply of ammunition arrived. Following the delivery, a new attack was launched, this time with Captain von der Malsburg operating on the right side (east) of West Road. Although eager to charge the American battery, the Hessians reached the emplacements but ran into stronger resistance than anticipated. Enroute they received fierce fire from houses and walls killing Captain von der Malsburg's pet dog that had been following him faithfully. At this point, von der Malsburg for the first time saw many blacks fighting for the rebels, whom he stated were not wearing jackets and were firing from behind walls. Posted in a grove in the valley, these men successfully warded off three Hessian attempts to break through their lines, contributing a great deal to the day's outcome. All the while, Hessian cannon were firing from Turkey Hill, their loud thunder encouraging the troops to keep moving forward.

Major General von Lossberg, on Turkey Hill with the left wing of the army, ordered the von Huyn Regiment, the Seybothen Regiment, and the King's Rangers to assist in providing fluidity to the advance on the enemy's positions. He was warned by a British dragoon, however, that a large force was moving toward Malsburg's left flank. This move resulted in a fighting withdrawal to Turkey Hill. By then the open combat had lasted for nine hours. The British-Hessian line of defense was now firmly established as running across the island in a line that included Quaker, Turkey, and Anthony Hills. At that time Major General von Lossberg ordered the von Ditfurth and Landgrave Regiments, which had been held in reserve, into the lines to bring his field force up to maximum strength.

At approximately 10:00 am, four British ships took up positions in the waters opposite a newly built American redoubt on the high ground of their defensive right wing. This favorable positioning of the ships enabled ground troops to operate under the umbrella of their guns, prompting Hessian attacks against Sullivan's right flank. The Rev. Manassah Cutler, pastor of the Congregational Church in Hamilton, Massachusetts, was in that area at the time. He noted in part that:

> The day was passed in skirmishing, and towards evening a body of the enemy had pushed our right wing and advanced so far as to endanger themselves. He attributed successful repulsive action to Colonel John Trumbull. He went on to say:

Oblique aerial view of the western end of the battle field in Portsmouth, Rhode Island. *Courtesy Portsmouth Abbey [Portsmouth, RI]*

As I rose to the crest of the hill I saw German troops who had just been repulsed, in evident disorder, endeavoring to reform their line, but fatigued. The Americans stopped their advance behind a strong wall, and without order grounded their weapons or leaned them against the fence.

According to articles that appeared in the *Bayreuther Zeitungen* during the latter part of 1778, General von Lossberg cited the excellent performance of the Ansbach (Ansbach-Bayreuth Regiment) Corps, and observed that the troops had remained under arms during the night following their day-long battle, and were prepared to dislodge the enemy the following morning. The reporter further noted that: "Men that had been in other wars did not recall such heavy and persistent cannon fire. By evening we were running out of ammunition, so we let them fire on us without responding."

According to Lieutenant MacKenzie, the British-Hessian troop alignment at that time placed the flanking companies of the 22nd and 54th Regiments on the easternmost end of the line, with the

43rd and Brown's Regiment at the crossroads, and Fanning's Regiment to their left as far as Turkey Hill. The First Ansbach was behind Turkey Hill with their left extending to West Road. The Second Ansbach (Bayreuth), von Ditfurth, von Huyn, and Landgrave Regiments were on line on the left side of West Road. The rock near Anthony's House was mentioned by MacKenzie as being on the line with the latest Hessian deployment. The chasseurs were assigned to the far left facing the bay.

As night fell upon the exhausted soldiers of both armies, their sentinels were posted in the fields—only 300 to 400 feet from each other. Observations made on the morning of August 30th showed the Americans still lodged in their positions, although some movement of the troops toward Howland's Ferry was reported.

WHAT NEXT?

General Pigot had been advised by some of his senior officers the night before to fall back to their earlier positions in Newport as a precautionary measure in the event Major General Sullivan decided to counterattack in force. However, he elected to hold the line, because he believed the enemy would attack in forty-eight hours, or abandon the island altogether. Pigot preferred to wait it out. In the meantime, work was initiated for a new redoubt to be built on the right flank of the defensive line, which seemed to be the weakest point in the alignment of his forces.

Later observations during the day following the battle seemed to indicate that the enemy was making definite moves to evacuate the island. Many troops, carts loaded with equipment, and even cattle, were heading for the ferry landing at Howland's Point. Despite this evident withdrawal, observations showed that the Americans were also continuing to strengthen their positions, and their artillery kept shelling Turkey Hill intermittently. The British responded in kind, hoping to knock out the enemy's guns, but without success. A report was received later in the day claiming the only troops the enemy had left on the island were colonials. Taken together, the various reports and sightings seemed to indicate Major General Sullivan was indeed withdrawing his forces from the island. At about 10:00 p.m. on August 30th, the sounds of oars and the movement of boats in the water near Howland's Ferry, combined with much talking coming from the same direction, prompted Major

General Prescott to check things out personally. By midnight many lights had been lit near the shore by the enemy while those on Butts Hill were being doused. By the following morning the evacuation of the island had been completed. A British scouting party entered the fortified area on Butts Hill without coming into contact with any enemy personnel. Soon after, General Pigot ordered various troop movements to effect the reoccupation of the northern end of Rhode Island, which had been vacated several weeks earlier when the French fleet was standing off Newport.

Hessian Reenactors at Windmill Hill (Butts Hill). *Courtesy Earle N. Trickey*

CHAPTER 18

After the Battle

COMMON SOLDIER'S ASSESSMENT

A comment in the diary of Johann Conrad Döhla of the Ansbach-Bayreuth contingent sums up the general attitude among his comrades following the withdrawal of Major General Sullivan's troops, when he wrote on August 29, 1778: "A most favorable day because a much larger force had to yield to the courage and bravery of our much smaller force."

While many of his fellows-in-arms will have felt as he did, Döhla, a young common soldier, may not have given much thought to the fact that the majority of General Sullivan's troops had not been regulars, but short-term enlistees with limited prior military training, nor that some were leaving the ranks as soon as their enlistment terms had expired no matter where they may have been assigned to duty. Sullivan is quoted as having said that he had been "inclined to attack the British and Germans, but his troops were hungry and tired." Also, he "only had 1,500 seasoned soldiers; the remainder were fresh recruits."

RELIEF AND CRITICISMS

On September 1, Sir Henry Clinton and Major General Grey sailed into Narragansett Bay with seventy ships carrying some 4,000 British soldiers plus naval crews intended to reinforce or even rescue the Newport garrison that had been under siege by the enemy. According to Lieutenant MacKenzie, the entire fleet was anchored in Newport harbor off Conanicut Island, but the troops were not ordered to disembark. Instead, General Clinton, after being given an up-to-date briefing, decided to depart with his fleet on

September 3. He was disappointed at not having been able to dislodge the enemy personally with the troops he had brought along, and was critical of British operations in breaking the siege. Of particular concern was Pigot's advance without the use of flank guards. This oversight had resulted in being ambushed by the enemy, that caused heavy casualties. Apparently a group of rebels had also been mistakenly identified as Hessians. Their true identity did not become known to the British until they were fired on at short range. Sir Henry Clinton criticized General Pigot, particularly for pursuing the enemy, knowing all along that his fleet with reinforcements was enroute. In addition, he felt General Pigot should have returned to his lines in Newport rather than risk his whole army in the event of a successful rebel counterattack. Negative remarks notwithstanding, he praised the bravery and endurance of the soldiers, commending the Germans in particular.

Reporting on troop behavior, Lieutenant MacKenzie noted:

> The excesses which have been committed on the island by all the troops since the 29th of August, have been very great and have thrown great disgrace on our arms. Sufficient pains have not been taken to stop them. One inhabitant was killed on the 29th by some of the Ansbachers who, entering the house from whence the rebels had been driven, took him for one of them and immediately shot him. The man was a poor inoffensive Quaker, and he left a wife and two children.

CASUALTIES

In reporting on the status of the King's troops, Lieutenant MacKenzie mentioned that the number of wounded Hessians in his opinion, was not as great as reported. He gave the following reasons for his statement:

> The Landgrave by the treaty is allowed so much for every man killed, and every three men wounded are reckoned as a man killed. The Captain of a Company is also allowed by the Landgrave so much for each man of his Company who is wounded; it is therefore in the interest of both to have the Return (report) swelled as much as possible. On these occasions they return (report) every man wounded who has had blood drawn.

While the alleged malpractice might have benefitted the Hessian princes, the meticulous military recordkeeping described earlier leaves some doubt that such fraudulent reports could have been endorsed and passed by the senior Hessian commanders.

Very controversial casualty figures develop when attempting to reconcile reports of claimed enemy losses as given by British/Hessian and American sources respectively. For instance, the *Providence Gazette* of September 5th, 1778 reported that "the enemy lost 1,023 men killed, wounded and taken." Sullivan's losses were concurrently listed as "upward of 700."

In a letter of August 31, 1778, appearing in the *Bayreuther Zeitungen*, General Pigot stated that only a few men had been taken prisoner, and that the enemy dead were greater in numbers than the royal troops. In total, he claimed 35 dead and 192 wounded among his officers and men. Later researchers increased his figures by including Hessian losses, to a total of 260. Even this count is unreliable when considering the Hessians' own reports. Still, whatever total is ultimately reached, it does not approach the 1,023 claimed in the *Providence Gazette*.

In a communication to his superiors, dated December 6th, Major General von Lossberg reported in part: "During the retreat of the rebels and our pursuit, we lost altogether 231 men, including English, Hessian, and Ansbach troops, comprising dead, wounded, captured, and missing personnel." He noted further, that the British 22nd Regiment on the right flank and von Huyn on the left, along with the avant guard led by Captains Malsburg and Noltenius had suffered the heaviest casualties.

Lossberg was apparently so chagrined by General Sullivan's report to Congress and the many plaudits the American was receiving for his successful withdrawal from the island, that he continued: "Sullivan in his report to Congress made a lot of noise about having annihilated us so we left more than 1,000 men on the battlefield... All men are liars—this man is no exception."

For their respective units, the Journals of the von Ditfurth and von Huyn Regiments each list a total of approximately fifty to sixty wounded and twenty-five dead. Among the troops from Ansbach-Bayreuth six were killed on the battlefield, and nine additional deaths were recorded after the battle, most of whom are assumed to have perished as a result of their wounds.

Past accounts of the Battle of Rhode Island include statements that some forty Hessians were laid to rest in a common grave on or near the battlefield where they fell. At one time the grave was appropriately marked, but over time the marker disappeared obliterating the burial site. There exist some Rhode Island maps of Portsmouth that identify a "Hessian's Hole" along Bloody Run Brook, in a swampy area not too far from Freeborn's Lane where the advancing Hessians encountered Sullivan's entrenched forces. To keep the memory of this historic area alive, the golf course of the exclusive Carnegie Abbey Golf Club, which embraces much of the former battlefield, has named the sixth hole as "Hessian's Hole."

THE FALL AND WINTER OF 1778

The period immediately following the withdrawal of Major General Sullivan's forces, though by no means a time for complacency, was a time when letter-writing was high on the agenda. Two letters, in particular, penned by Captain von der Malsburg at Elam's Farm to Lieutenant-General von Ditfurth under the dates of September 6 and November 16, 1778, provide an idea of the inner thoughts of this officer whose performance during the Battle of Rhode Island was widely heralded:

September 6 ... After having safely escaped from many dangers that menaced us, and been delivered from the French fleet that enclosed us for some time and the hostile army that besieged us, I now seize my pen... I am longing to pay humble respects to your Excellency in person, but this hope seems more distant than ever, if England will not agree to the Independence of America and withdraw the troops... We shall await our fate upon what the two fleets undertake. The French being repaired in Boston threaten to pay us another visit here on Rhode Island.

November 16 ...It is strange that England and France are fighting against each other without any previous declaration of war. The behavior of the French amounts to such a declaration [in his opinion]... The latest proposals made by the Commissioners of Peace who were sent from England, have again been

> rejected by Congress, however advantageous they may have been... These unhappy people cannot in any way be dissuaded from demanding their entire separation from England; but whether they will live happily when thus separated, and enjoy a dismembered government, is still very doubtful.

When General Clinton departed Narragansett Bay, General Grey, who had accompanied him, set out for New Bedford with a landing force and there burnt and destroyed a large number of sailing ships. In the Newport area, British and Hessian troops busily dismantled many of the American earthworks that had been erected during the siege. Supplies for the coming winter became another matter of concern for the garrison, and some 5,000 sheep were brought in from Martha's Vineyard in mid-September. Soon after, efforts were made to mine coal not far from Easton's Beach. Lieutenant MacKenzie notes that it produced nothing more than culm that would burn but was difficult to ignite. He thought a shaft deeper than the twenty feet the troops had dug would be required.

General Pigot, who had been well liked, departed Newport on September 28 and General Prescott took over his command. A detail of Ansbach-Bayreuth recruits arrived a few days before Pigot's departure and was assigned to the regiment, at that time stationed at Butts (Windmill) Hill. Chaplain George Erb, who arrived with the recruits, preached his first sermon on October 18. When that regiment moved to its winter quarters in Newport toward the end of November, the chaplain conducted religious services at the Quaker Meeting House.

Prior to his departure at the beginning of September, General Clinton made it known that he would once again like to see an operational battery situated at the Dumplings to replace the defenses that had been abandoned and the guns that were thrown over the cliff, when the French fleet initially approached. Following up on Clinton's wishes, General Prescott visited Conanicut Island on October 1 and directed that a battery of four large guns and a redoubt for fifty men be built. Anticipating a possible rebel landing on Conanicut Island, Brown's detachment was sent to reinforce the British marines that had relieved the 54th Regiment and had been assigned to the island soon after the siege had ended.

British Sketch of the Dumplins and plan for a battery of four guns.
Clements Library, University of Michigan, Ann Arbor, MI

Firewood for the coming winter months became a matter of grave concern that had to be dealt with. Lieutenant MacKenzie estimated 400 cord of wood would be required per week, or 10,000 cord in twenty-five weeks. As of October 5, the garrison had 1,500 cord on hand, with approximately 2,000 more that could be acquired on the island. In due course, all existing trees, many fences, vacant houses and barns, docks, and abandoned boats were taken and eventually consumed to heat the requisitioned living spaces in the town of Newport during the winter months.

The winter of 1778–1779 was one of the coldest ever. This opinion was voiced by Lieutenant MacKenzie, and seconded by entries found in the *Journal of the von Ditfurth Regiment*. MacKenzie reported on Christmas Day, 1778, that the bay was smoking like fog; wine froze in its bottles as did mustard and pickles. Poultry died of frostbite and a shortage of food required that bread be made from rice and flour. A storm the following day deposited eighteen inches of snow. Strong wind caused very high drifts. The accompanying temperatures and frost made it dangerous to be outside. Twenty-foot drifts were reported at the time, some requiring people to leave their houses by way of a second floor window to find and dig out their front doors. Roads were impassable for horses and carriages. For December 26, 1778, the von Ditfurth Journal reads in part:

> Terrible snow storm; none like it remembered by the oldest inhabitants of the island. Three men from Regiment von Bünau died in the blizzard. Aside from the extreme weather, the regiments were short on provisions, especially bread which was almost nonexistent. Instead, bread was made from rice and spoiled oat flour which could not be consumed.

CHAPTER 19

1779: Time to Leave

DESPERATE TIMES

The extreme winter weather experienced during the latter part of 1778 continued well into the first months of 1779. By then, a large percentage of the six- to seven-thousand troops on Rhode Island had been pulled into Newport so they might find protection from the elements in weathertight quarters. The prevailing shortage of firewood and the resultant inability of the troops to "keep the fires burning," made garrison life challenging and sometimes even unpleasant. Men on duty at remote outposts died from exposure, and the food supply was dwindling. The situation had become more deplorable by the day.

Fortunately, resupply ships from New York arrived on January 18. Loyalists who had formed a militia unit aided the desperate garrison by venturing to the mainland, where they rounded up and brought back 300 head of cattle. Despite their commendable efforts, meat rations had to be cut back considerably and dried fish and salt substituted. By May, the garrison's food supplies were exhausted. In an attempt to maintain troop morale, a beer substitute was created made out of wood, molasses, and herbs that were boiled into a syrup-like consistency. The resultant sweet tea-like drink could by no imagination take the place of beer. Some of the men suffered upset stomachs from consuming the concoction. Because of a desperate shortage of flour, bread was made from oats, peas, and Turkish cornmeal. Many food improvisations came about after Dr. Schöpp, a regimental surgeon, arrived from New York on January 11, 1779. To help alleviate the food shortage, he ordered the planting of vegetables. In so doing, he was later able to improve the diet for hospitalized personnel.

DUTY AS USUAL

The many hardships that confronted the Hessians and their British comrades had to be overcome within the bounds of the given circumstances. Captain von der Malsburg's journal reflects the praises and compliments paid by their General Lossberg on the good behavior of the Ansbach Corps, commanded by Colonel de Voit, and of Captains Malsburg and Noltenius and their companies of Chasseurs.

General Lossberg's January 18, 1779 letter to Lieutenant-General von Ditfurth at Marburg includes the following: "Captain Noltenius of the Bünau Regiment, even though wounded on August 29th, has every hope of recovering even though he still has a musket-ball in his body." He went on to report that Noltenius had hemorrhaged and broken his diaphragm, and that he had been attended by English, Hessian, and Ansbach physicians. Lossberg included a personal plea that the Landgrave support Noltenius since he will no longer be able to continue his military service.

General Lossberg also reported that his troops were now eating mostly barley broth and little else, and that very few cattle were left for consumption. Thieves among the troops were punished by making them run the gauntlet.

During the last days of March, General von Bose of the Landgrave Regiment received orders to assume command of the von Trümbach Regiment. Shortly after, he departed Newport in the company of the British 26th Light Infantry Regiment. He was replaced in Newport by Major General von Kosputh who took command of the Landgrave Regiment at that time.

The *Journal of Leib-Infantry Regiment von Wutgenau* notes on February 2 that the Frigate *Talion*, which had been sunk when the French fleet approached, had been raised and repaired. Two weeks later, the man-of-war *Raisonnable* moved into the harbor coming from the West Channel and then departed with the guard ship *Renown* to meet and escort Admiral Gambier, who was coming to assess the local situation.

On his arrival in Newport on March 16th, Admiral Gambier received a thirteen-gun salute in his honor. General Pattison,

General Matthews, and Commissary General Wien accompanied Admiral Gambier during his inspection, which ended when Gambier departed a week later.

The *Diary of Johann Ernst Prechtel* (a Lieutenant in the Ansbach-Bayreuth Regiment) noted on March 21 that two new forts were laid out on Conanicut Island. The first, known as Fort Brown, was situated close to the channel, and Fort Green, the second, sited in the middle of the island. A plan for the latter reads in part: "Redoubt erected at Conanicut 700 yards from East Ferry, 750 from West, defending the Isthmus of Beaver Tail, the North Causeway and the East Ferry, for sixty-eight men."

On April 11 when it appeared the enemy was making preparations to launch an attack on Brown's Corps of Provincials stationed on Conanicut Island, the British 43rd Regiment was sent to reinforce the island detail. The von Wutgenau Journal contains a notation to the effect that the enemy had at that time assembled 120 flat-bottomed boats at Narragansett. A landing on Conanicut Island was not attempted, however. A month later, on May 28 Colonel Fanning's Regiment of Provincials also set up camp on Conanicut Island.

A second move to reduce the size of the Newport garrison got underway on June 11 when the Landgrave Regiment, the British 54th Regiment and the Fanning Corps of Provincials were ordered to make preparations for an early departure from Rhode Island. Five days later, the troops marched through Newport to the cadence of their drums and with their Regimental colors flying high. Following their arrival at the wharves, the troops boarded their designated transports, and the fleet, consisting of forty ships, headed for the open water by way of Brenton's Point and Conanicut Island. Sudden high winds forced the convoy to anchor and wait for calmer weather. It was not until June 25 that the fleet finally got underway. The *Journal of Regiment von Wutgenau*, in telling of the voyage, mentions hearing the sound of gunfire as they "passed that robber's nest, New London."

During the time the above units were gearing up to be transported to another duty station, the von Huyn Regiment participated in the burial ceremony for Major von Arnberg, who had fallen from a wagon several weeks earlier and died of his injuries on June 23.

Lieutenant Johann Ernst Prechtel made the following record for June 24:

> In quarters in Newport. Major von Arnberg, who died yesterday, was buried today in the churchyard of the English (Trinity) Church. A detachment of 150 men of the Hessian Huyn Regiment fired three volleys.

The loss of one British regiment in March 1779 due to transfer, and the departure of two additional regiments (one Hessian and one British) plus the Fanning Corps in June, considerably reduced the defensive capabilities of the remaining occupation forces. It is understandable then, that the rebels dared to make a brazen landing at Brenton Point during the night of June 27 in an attempt to seize some livestock.

It appears that Admiral Gambier's findings from his earlier inspection and assessment of conditions in the Narragansett Bay area may have triggered the gradual pullout of troops during subsequent months.

The complete abandonment of Newport followed when more than fifty ships arrived on October 11 with orders to evacuate the garrison. Baggage was soon readied and collected for shipment, while many of the garrison's personnel were kept busy demolishing their batteries, strong-points, and magazines. On October 25, the regiments struck their respective camps and marched to the dock with their drums beating and their flags waving in the wind. General Prescott ordered all windows to be kept shut and the citizenry to stay inside their houses while the troops were moving through the streets. He is said to have issued the order to insure that his men would not be induced by the population to desert and remain behind.

The British fleet that evacuated all of the King's men and their Hessian partners also provided transportation for forty-two Tory families when they sailed from the shores of Rhode Island on the evening of October 25, 1779.

PLAUDITS

Prior to his departure from Newport, Major General John Christoph von Huyn was thanked and praised in a proclamation issued by a number of citizens for the discipline he maintained among his troops. Following is the translation of that communication as it appears in the *Journal of Garrison-Regiment von Huyn*:

> By the Desire of the Inhabitants of Rhode Island to Major General de Huyn, commanding the British and Hessian troops from Bavia Gate to Bristol Ferry –
>
> May it please your Excellency, to accept the most grateful thanks of the inhabitants for the humanity with which they have been treated since your Excellency took the Command and be assured Sir, they are sensible, that a father would not, with more patience, have heard the complaints of his children, than your Excellency, nor more effectually than Your Excellency has endeavored to do by keeping the troops under your Command in the utmost discipline and good order imaginable.
>
> Be assured, Sir, in losing Your Excellency, we lose a gentleman under whose protection and command we have been as happy as those times would permit, and that Your Excellency may return home to your native country, laden with riches and honour, and at least your Grey hair may descend to the grave in peace beloved and respected by Prince and People, which is the sincere Wishes of Your Excellencies most obedient servants, the subscribers.
>
> Rhode Island the 12th of October 1779.

Samuel Allen	Elisha Allen
Pill Allen	Wm. Brown
Gideon Brown	Joseph Martin
Saram William	Elisab. Jipson
Jonas Coggshall	John Slokum ser.
Jonathan Coggshall	George Cornel
Elisha Coggshall	Gelly Slokum ser.
John Coggshall	Thom. Manchester
John Coggshall	Walter Radmann
Josua Coggshall	
John Slokum jun.	
Pallec Manchester	
Thom. Wiwer sen.	

Thom. Wiwer jun.
Gideon Coggshall
Thom. Coggshall
John Coggshall
George Lowton
Peter Taylor
Isaac Manchester
Elisab. Goding

Note 1: The spelling of the above names is as they appear in the typed archival translation of the handwritten German original.

Note 2: General von Huyn replied by letter of October 15, 1779, accepting the plaudits and advising that the inhabitants "may depend on every indulgence that can be granted by General Prescott."

Note 3: General von Huyn died in New York on July 26, 1780.

HONORS

Captain Friedrich von der Malsburg, in a letter written at Huntington, Long Island, on November 6, 1779, and addressed to his superior, Lieutenant-General von Ditfurth at Marburg, had this to say regarding a decoration he received:

> ...I found the Order waiting in New York, and Lieutenant-General von Knyphausen personally hung it around my neck. I know, your Excellency had the greatest share in my receiving the above, and I therefore wish to tender my dutiful and most humble thanks to your Excellency for it.

COMPLIMENTING THE ENEMY

Appearing in the *Bayreuther Zeitungen* on June 17, 1779, Major General Grey, observes:

> The Americans showed us they are soldiers and not just farmers. They built redoubts all around us, except for the side facing the water, dug trenches, drove us out of our camps with their cannon fire and had the will to storm our lines. But, this was the one thing their volunteers wanted to avoid, and just as well, for they would have lost many men without a fleet to support them. Their retreat was well planned and executed orderly.

1779: Time to Leave

Lost Time

After being returned to New York, the Hessian units of the abandoned Newport garrison received various new location assignments. For instance, Fusilier Regiment von Ditfurth and a part of Garrison Regiment von Huyn were transferred to Charleston, while the Ansbach-Bayreuth units went on to serve in Virginia for a period of time. Musketeer Regiment von Wutgenau saw service in New York. The two chasseur companies that distinguished themselves so well during the Battle of Rhode Island had been disbanded on November 25, 1778 and the men returned to their original regiments. Some of the troops from among those having served in Newport were later interned for a period of time following the surrender of General Cornwallis at Yorktown in October 1781.

By 1783, all of the Hessian and Franconian (Ansbach-Bayreuth) troops were returned to German ports for disembarkation, from whence they once again trekked across land that was more familiar to most of them, on their way back to their families and the garrison cities they had not seen for six to seven years. Prayers for their safe return from the war had been offered in officially sanctioned decrees endorsed by their princes.

The Surrender of General Cornwallis at Yorktown. *Author's Collection*

Gebetsformel

um glückliche Ruckreise der nach erfolgten Frieden

aus America

zurückgehenden

Hochfürstlich Brandenburgischen Truppen

welche

auf immediaten Befehl

Ihro Hochfürstlichen Durchlaucht

vom

Hochfürstl. Consistorio zu Bayreuth

den Geistlichen des Obergebürgischen Fürstenthums, bey dem öffentlichen Gottesdienst abzulesen vorgeschrieben worden 1783.

Prayer for safe return of Brandenburg troops. *Courtesy Horst Lochner*

Losses

Approximately two-thirds of the original troop contingent sent to America eventually returned to their homes in Germany. The number of personnel killed in action is comparatively small when compared to the large number of men who deserted (in particular during the last years of the war) or elected to stay in America after hostilities ceased. In addition, a greater number of deaths among the troops is attributable to sickness, harsh weather here, or fever, rather than battle-related causes. Total attrition (failure to return or be returned) approaches 12,000 for Hessians and Ansbach-Bayreuthers combined.

CHAPTER 20

Concluding Thoughts

Who Won?

When two forces compete against each other, be it in sports or war, there is the presumption that such a match or campaign will produce a winner. In a ball game the outcome is very conclusive and the winning teams continue on through additional phases of peaceful competition. In a life-and-death situation as in a war, the victor prevails and imposes his will on the defeated opponent who will bow his head in humility. There are situations however, that do not produce a clear winner and the end result may be a withdrawal, an armistice, a truce—or perhaps a simple draw for want of a better word. The latter possibility could save face, putting aside any admission of having lost, nor opening a debate on a shaky declaration of victory.

In the American Revolution, there is no doubt that the American forces emerged as the undisputed victors following the surrender of their British and Hessian opponents at Yorktown in 1781. The formation of the United States of America, independent of foreign domination, is proof of that outcome.

However, various points of view have been voiced regarding the outcome of the Battle of Rhode Island. The positions taken by various historians and writers are presented here to provide the reader with a range of thoughts that could serve to support declaring either side the winner or loser, or perhaps rating the outcome as "undecided." Following are excerpts from the declarations of these sources which may be worthy of further thought and consideration:

"The successful outcome of the American Revolution made it difficult to secure a patient hearing of the other side." "The battle was a rear guard action as the Americans extracted their troops from Aquidneck when French naval support failed to materialize..." "Next day the enemy abandoned the island." "After failure of operations against Newport, General Sullivan resumed his post in Providence." "Realizing the siege was doomed, Sullivan withdrew northward to Portsmouth with British and Hessians in pursuit... If the rebels had been overrun, Sullivan's entire army would have been captured." "Sullivan's troops got away... the retreat was prudent, timely, and well conducted." "A general attack in coordination with the French was planned but thwarted by the arrival of Howe's fleet." "The enemy departed by boat during the night, leaving the entire island to the British and Hessians. General Clinton came with help, but too late, the rebels had left the island."

Notwithstanding these accounts, the British and Hessians held on to Newport after the August 1778 battle until they themselves decided to evacuate all of Rhode Island in October of the following year. Their departure was voluntary, although hanging on to their prized Rhode Island possessions was becoming economically unfeasible. British and Hessian troops were tied down and confined to Rhode Island where they were effectively neutralized, and no longer a viable force capable of impacting the colonists on the mainland. Simply said, they could not dare venture from their home base with the limited resources available to them without endangering their very own existence. And keeping the combined British-Hessian garrison supplied from without had become a pressing problem that weighed heavily on the British command.

Robert Wheeler may have summed it up pretty well when he made his calculated statement that the first combined operation of American and French arms was a fizzle and that the Battle of Rhode Island was a "draw."

A better assessment might be that the five-week siege of Newport was unsuccessful, but, that General Sullivan prevailed in the Battle of Rhode Island by repulsing the attackers repeatedly, forcing them to retire to Turkey and Quaker Hills. This enabled Sullivan to successfully evacuate his troops from Aquidneck Island without futher losses.

Concluding Thoughts

Reminders

To envision what it must have been like during the British-Hessian occupation of Newport and Rhode Island could require considerable research to produce an understanding of the places frequented or used by the foreign troops. One interesting category of accessible remains are the earthworks that were built at the time, and monuments that were erected later to memorialize certain events.

Though not well maintained, Butts Hill in Portsmouth is one of the larger sites occupied by American, British, and Hessian troops at different times during the three-year occupation of Rhode Island. A nearby overlook facing west on Route 114 (West Main Road), provides an excellent view of that section of the battlefield where Hessian and Franconian soldiers and the special chasseur units met up with General Sullivan's forces as they made their stand, backs to the Sakonnet River. The fields where the Hessians attempted to charge the American lines are now owned by the Carnegie Abbey Golf Club. A monument honoring the Black Regiment is located in close proximity.

Memorial to the Black Regiment. *Author's Photo*

Several sites in Newport also bring Revolutionary War history to life. North Battery, situated at the foot of the Newport Bridge is readily accessible, so is Green End Fort, near Simmons Court. The highest elevation in Miantonomi Park, with its stone tower and flag, is another site that had been heavily fortified during the 1776–1779 period. In those days the area was referred to as Tonomy Hill by the Hessians. Fort Adams, off Harrison Avenue, was built on the site of an earlier Revolutionary War earthworks.

The site of Green End Fort is well maintained and identified with this granite marker. *Author's Photo*

Within the historic area of downtown Newport there are many buildings and structures that existed before British and Hessian forces landed in December 1776. Among these are: Thames Street; Friend's Meeting House, 1699; White Horse Tavern, 1673; Wanton-Lyman-Hazard House, 1699; the Colony House, 1739–42; Brick Market, 1762; Touro Synagogue, 1763; Redwood Library, 1748;

Concluding Thoughts

Vernon House, 1750; Sabbatarian Meeting House, 1729; Trinity Church, 1726; Bowens Wharf, 1700; Hunter House, 1748, and others. Realizing that these same buildings were noticed, admired, and written about by the occupiers gives them a special place in local history, and knowing that these buildings remain to this day makes it worth trying to envision them in their earlier settings.

Lost for many years, this marker donated by the Daughters of the American Revolution in 1931, was reinstalled at Conanicut Battery in 2003. *Author's Photo*

Conanicut Island, or Jamestown as it is properly called, is the site of the oft-mentioned Beaver Tail Battery, now commonly known as Conanicut Battery. Strategically located along the western shore of Beavertail, this well-kept earthworks allows the mind to wander as one envisions the British fleet of 75–80 ships sailing up the West Passage on December 6, 1776 to effect the occupation of Newport with more than 6,000 troops.

Return of the French

It had been devastating for General Sullivan to see the French fleet under Comte d'Estaing leave Narragansett Bay, at a time when he had hoped to launch a coordinated attack on Newport with the support of several thousand French troops. His calculated with-

Conanicut Battery with interpretive sign in 2005. *Author's Photo*

drawal from the outskirts of Newport and the immediate pursuit by troops of the British-Hessian garrison did little to brighten his day. Still, he was able to break the momentum of their advance in the vicinity of Butts Hill at the northern end of Rhode Island, enabling him to save his troops by moving them back to their original jump-off point across the water in Tiverton without any significant interference. That feat was on August 29–30, 1778. A year later, on October 25, 1779, the British and Hessians evacuated Newport.

Then suddenly, on July 10, 1780, the masts of a large armada was spotted on the horizon by Newporters. The ships were identified as French. It turned out that an expeditionary force of 5,800 men under command of Jean-Baptiste-Donatien de Vimeur, Comte de Rochambeau, had finally arrived. The troops consisted primarily of infantry regiments Royal Deux-Ponts, Soissonnais, Bourbonnais and Saintonge. The interesting part is that the Royal Deux-Ponts Regiment took its name from Zweibrücken, an independent German-speaking duchy in what is the Rhineland today. Of course, when these German-speaking French troops disembarked in Newport, the locals did not quite understand what was happening. Were the Hessians back? Any misunderstandings were soon clarified for all concerned. The French remained in Newport until June

12, 1781, when they broke camp and marched to Philadelphia by way of Providence, Hartford, and West Point. They participated in the actions that culminated in the American victory over the British at Yorktown. Prior to the march, General Washington came to Newport on March 6, 1781, where he met with Rochambeau.

FINAL WORDS

In assessing the true character of the Hessians, in particular officers like those who served in Newport during the period 1776–1779, the comments of two historians are worthy of note:

George Washington Greene (1876): "Men whose names might have stood high in the annals of war, if they had fought for their country, are known in history as fighters for hire."

J.G. Rosengarten (1886): "Many who served in America, were men of distinction in later life and much of the excellence that marked the German armies in their own war of freedom against France was acquired in their earlier service in America."

A tribute to those who died in the Battle of Rhode Island.
Courtesy Narragansett Bay Carnegie Abbey

Bibliography

Almy, Mary. "Mrs. Almy's Journal. Siege of Newport, R.I., August, 1778." *Newport Historical Magazine 1* (1880-1).

Amory, Thomas C. *The Military Services and Public Life of Major-General John Sullivan of the American Revolutionary Army.* Boston: Wiggin and Lunt, 1868.

Ansbach-Bayreuther Truppen im Nordamerikanischen Unabhängigkeitskrieg 1777-1783 (Kleine Ausstellung des Kriegsarchivs Nr. 57), by Bayerisches Hauptstaatsarchiv, Abteilung IV Kriegsarchiv. Munich: Andreas R. Bräunling, 1997.

Archambault, Florence. *"Forward Through the Ages, in Unbroken Line": 300 Years of Congregationalism on Aquidneck Island, 1695-1995.* Middletown, Rhode Island: United Congregational Church in Newport, 1995.

Arnold, Samuel Greene. *History of the State of Rhode Island and Providence Plantations.* vol. 2. New York: D. Appleton & Co., 1860.

Arnold, Samuel Greene, Max von Eelking, and John Sullivan. *The Centennial Celebration of the Battle of Rhode Island at Portsmouth, Rhode Island, August 29, 1878.* Providence: S. Rider, 1878.

Asteroth aus Treysa, Johann Valentine. *Das Tagebuch des Sockenstrickers Johann Valentin Asteroth aus Treysa, Stadtgeschichtlicher Arbeitskreis e.V.* Edited by Heinz Krause. Schwalmstadt-Treysa, 1992.

Atwood, Rodney. *The Hessians: Mercenaries from Hessen-Kassel in the American Revolution.* New York: Cambridge University Press, 1980.

Auerbach, Inge. *Die Hessen in Amerika 1776-1783*. Darmstadt: Hessische Historische Kommission Darmstadt; Marburg: Historische Kommission für Hessen Marburg, 1996.

Auerbach, Inge and Otto Fröhlich. *Hessiche Truppen im Amerikanischen Unabhängigkeitskrieg*. vols. 14. Marburg: Archiveschule Marburg, 1976, 1984, 1987.

Baker, Virginia. *The History of Warren, Rhode Island, in the War of The Revolution, 1776-1783*. Warren, Rhode Island, 1901. Reprint by Salem, Massachusetts: Higginson Book Company, 1998.

Baurmeister, Carl Leonard. *Revolution in America: Confidential Letters and Journals, 1776-1784 of Adjutant General Major Baurmeister of the Hessian Forces*. Edited and translated by Bernard A. Uhlendorf. New Brunswick, New Jersey: Rutgers University Press, 1957.

Bayreuther Zeitungen (1776-1779), excerpts from Archives of Unibibliothek, Bayreuth, Germany. Transcribed by Horst Lochner, Bayreuth, July 2001.

Bezzel, Oskar. "Ansbach-Bayreuther Miettruppen im Nordamerikanischen Freiheitskrieg 1777-1783." *Zeitschrift fur bayerische Landesgeschichte* 8 (1935): 185-214, 377-421.

Bockowitz [Regimental Quartermaster (German-English)] *Journal of Leib Infantry Regiment (von Wutginau), 1776 to May 1784*. Marburg: Hessen-Kasselisches Archiv, Fiche no. X 320-321.

Böhm, Uwe Peter. *Hessisches Militär: Die Truppen der Landgrafschaft Hessen-Kassel, 1672-1806*. Beckum, Germany: Vogel-Druck, 1986.

Carrington, Henry Beebee. *Battle Maps and Charts of the American Revolution*, 1887. Reprint by New York: Arno Press, 1974.

Chartrand, Rene. "Uniforms of Hesse-Cassel Troops." *Military Historian and Collector* no. 23 (Fall 1971): 90-91.

Conley, Patrick. *An Album of Rhode Island History, 1636-1986*. Norfolk, Virginia: Donning Company, 1986.

____. "The Battle of Rhode Island, 29 August 1778: A Victory for the Patriots." *Rhode Island History* 62, no. 3 (Fall 2004).

BIBLIOGRAPHY

Conley, Patrick, and Albert Klyberg. *Rhode Island's Road to Liberty, Bill of Rights*. Rhode Island Bicentennial Foundation. A selected documentary display aboard the H.M.S. Rose, on October 2-20, 1991.

Commager, Henry Steele, and Richard B. Morris, eds. *The Spirit of Seventy Six*. New York: Harper-Collins, 1967. Reprint, Edison, New Jersey: Castle Books, 2002.

The Company of Military Historians. *Military Uniforms in America: The Era of the American Revolution 1755-1795*. Edited by John Robert Elting (Col. USA ret.). San Rafael, California: Presidio Press, 1974.

Copeland, Peter F., and Albert W. Haarmann. "Provisional Chasseur Companies." *Military Historian and Collector* no. 18 (Spring 1966): 11-13.

Cöster, G.C. *Hessian Soldiers in the American Revolution: Records of their marriages and baptisms of their children in America, performed by the Rev. G.C. Cöster, 1776-1783, Chaplain of two Hessian Regiments*. Edited and translated by Marie Paula DickorÈ. Cincinnati: The C.J. Krehbiel Co., 1959.

Clermont-Crévecoeur, Jean Francois Louis, et al. *The American Campaigns of Rochambeaus Army, 1780, 1781, 1782, 1783*, 2 vols. Edited and translated by Howard C. Rice, Jr. and Anne S. K. Brown. Princeton, New Jersey: Princeton University Press, 1972.

Crane, Elaine Forman. *A Dependent People: Newport, Rhode Island in the Revolutionary Era*. New York: Fordham University Press, 1985.

Cruising Guide: Marine Advisory Service. Kingston: University of Rhode Island, 1976. Blaskowitz Map.

Dearden, Paul F. *The Rhode Island Campaign of 1778: Inauspicious Dawn of Alliance*. Providence: Rhode Island Publications Society in association with the Rhode Island Bicentennial Foundation, 1980.

Döhla, Johann Conrad. *A Hessian Diary of the American Revolution*. Edited and translated by Bruce E. Burgoyne from the 1913 Bayreuth edition by W. Baron von Waldenfels. Norman: University of Oklahoma Press, 1990.

Dornberg, Karl Ludwig and Gotthold Marseille. *Tagebuchblätter eines hessischen Offiziers aus der Zeit des Nordamerikanischen Unabhängigkeitskrieges.* 2 vols. Pyritz : Backesche Buchdruckerei, 1900.

Eelking, Max von. *Die Deutschen Hülfstruppen im Nordamerikanischen Befreiungskriege, 1776 bis 1783.* 2 vols. Hanover: Helwing, 1863.

____. *The German Allied Troops in the North American War of Independence, 1776-1783.* Edited and translated by J.G. Rosengarten. Albany, New York: J. Munsells Sons, 1893.

Elliot, George H., Lt. Col., Corps of Engineers. "Fort Greene Newport Harbor, Rhode Island" in *Report of Chief of Engineers, U.S. Army,* (January 15, 1885). Appendix no. 2, pp. 425–42.

Erb, Phillip Johann. *Erb aus Bayreuth, Feldprediger Johann Phillip. Feldkirchenregister, Regiment von Seybothen.* Ministry of St. Georgen, Bayreuth. Transcribed by Karl Walther, 1997.

Evans, Elizabeth. *Weathering the Storm: Women of the American Revolution.* New York: Scribner, 1975.

Ewald, Johann von. *Diary of the American War: A Hessian Journal.* Edited and translated by Joseph P. Tustin. New Haven: Yale University Press, 1979.

Field, Edward. *Revolutionary Defenses in Rhode Island: an historical account of the fortifications and beacons erected during the American revolution, with muster rolls of the companies stationed along the shores of Narragansett bay.* Providence: Preston and Rounds, 1896.

____. *State of Rhode Island and Providence Plantations at the End of a Century: A History.* vol. 1. Boston: Mason Publishing Company, 1902.

Freiheit für Amerika! Der Kampf um die amerikanische Unabhängigkeit, 1775-83. London: The British Museum Publications, for the Museum für Hamburgische Geschicte, 1976.

Garman, James E. *Historic Houses of Portsmouth, Rhode Island.* Newport: Franklin Printing House, 1976.

____. *A History of Portsmouth Rhode Island, 1638-1978.* Newport: Newport Historical Society, 1978.

Gesellschaft für Hessische Militär- und Zivilgeschichte e.V. "Vor 225 Jahren zogen Marburger und Frankenberger nach Amerika." http://www.hessen-militaer.de/aktuelles_thema.htm

"George III." *Encyclopedia Britannica,* 1987, 15th ed. Micropaedia vol. 5, p. 194.

Greene, George Washington. *The German Element in the War of American Independence.* New York: Hurd and Houghton, 1876.

Haarmann, Albert B. "Ansbach-Bayreuth Troops in North America" *Military Historian and Collector* no. 19 (Summer 1967): 48-49.

Hagist, Don N. *General Orders, Rhode Island; December 1776-January 1778.* Bowie, Maryland: Heritage Books, 2001.

Haley, John Williams. *The "Old Stone Bank" History of Rhode Island.* vol. 3. Providence: Providence Institution for Savings, 1939.

Handwerker, Otto. *Die Meuterei von Ochsenfurt,* Würzberg, 1935.

Hattendorf, John B. *Semper Eadem: A History of Trinity Church, 1698–2000.* Newport, RI: Trinity Church, 2001.

"Historical Preservation & Treatment Plan for Conanicut Battery on Prospect Hill, Jamestown, Rhode Island." *Landscapes* (Charlotte, VT, and Westport, CT) (February 1999).

Högler, Peter. *Die Ochsenfurter Revolte; 10. Murz 1777, Kreisheimatpfleger Peter Högler, Heimatpflege im Landkreis* Würzburg, Oellingen, Germany: Verlag Frankebund, 2002.

Holt, James W., Jr. *Fort Barton: Authentic Revolutionary War Redoubt.* Tiverton, Rhode Island.

Ingrao, Charles W. *The Hessian Mercenary State: Ideas, Institutions, and Reform under Frederick II, 1760–1785.* Cambridge and New York: Cambridge University Press, 1987.

Johnson, Charlotte Eschenheimer. "A New Perspective on Rose Island: The Evolution of its Fortifications and Defenses." *Newport History, Bulletin of the Newport Historical Society* 59, no. 201 (Winter 1986): 8.

Kappes, Johannes. "March Route from Hessen to America." *Journal of the Johannes Schwalm Historical Association* 7, no. 4 (2004).

Katcher, Philip R.N. *Encyclopedia of British, Provincial, and German Army Units, 1775-1783.* Harrisburg, Pennsylvania: Stackpole Books, 1973.

Kellner, George H., J. Stanley Lemons, and Linda Lotridge Levin. *Rhode Island: The Independent State.* Woodland Hills, California: Windsor Publications in association with Rhode Island Historical Society, 1982.

Kipping, Ernst. *The Hessian View of America 1776-1783.* Monmouth Beach, New Jersey: Philip Freneau Press, 1971.

Kleinschmidt , G. [Regimental Quartermaster (German-English)]. *Journal of Garrison Regiment Von Huyn (later Benning) 1776-mid 1783.* Marburg: Hessen-Kasselisches Archiv. Kriegssachen O.W.S. I.B.a.13, box 2436. Fiche T 299-303.

Knoetel, Herbert. "Hesse-Kassel Ditfurth Regiment." *Military Historian and Collector* no. 2 (March 1950): 1415.

Kopp, Andreas. "Die deutschen Truppen im amerikanischen Unabhängigkeitskrieg." *Modell Figuren* Berlin: Andreas Pietruschka, 2000.

Kügler, Dietmar. *Die deutschen Truppen im amerikanischen Unabhängigkeitskrieg 1775-1783.* Stuttgart: Motorbuch Verlag, 1980.

Laffin, John. *Jackboot: A History of the German Soldier, 1713-1945.* 1965. Reprint, New York: Barnes & Noble Books, 1994.

Learned, Marion Dexter. *Guide to the Manuscript Materials relating to American History in the German State Archives.* Washington, D.C.: Carnegie Institution of Washington, 1912.

Lefferts, Charles Mackubin, and Alexander J. Wall. *Uniforms of the American, British, French, and German Armies in the American Revolution, 1775-1783.* New York: New York Historical Society, 1926.

General Loßberg's letter to his Right Honorable and Esteemed Major General, December 6, 1778. William Clements Library, Ann Arbor, Michigan.

Low, William Gilman. "Beaver Tail Light, Conanicut, Rhode Island." *Bulletin of the Jamestown Historical Society* no. 7 (August 1936).

Lowell, Edward Jackson. *The Hessians and the other German Auxiliaries of Great Britain in the Revolutionary War*. 1884. Reprint, Williamstown, Massachusetts: Corner House Publishers, 1970.

MacKenzie, Frederick. *Diary of Frederick MacKenzie: giving a daily narrative of his military service as an officer of the regiment of Royal Welsh fusiliers during the years 1775-1781 in Massachusetts, Rhode Island, and New York*. 2 vols. Cambridge: Harvard University Press, 1930.

Malsburg, Friedrich Wilhelm von der. *Journal of Capt. Friedrich von der Malsburg, Regt. Ditfurth, Feb. 1777-Nov. 1780*. Edited and translated by Max von Eelking. Hanover, 1863.

_____. *Malsburg Diary (Excerpts from), Military Reports, Accounts of the Hessian Corps in America 1776-1780*. Staatsarchiv Marburg, Military Reports and Accounts, Fiche Nos. Letter Z.326-355.

_____. *Malsburg Diary (Excerpts from), Military Reports, Accounts of the Hessian Corps in America 1776-1780*. Staatsarchiv Marburg, 10E Kriegstageb‚cher I, Nr 1 18-1/2, BI-1-8I.

_____. *Letters & Others, to Lieutenant-General von Ditfurth at Marburg*. Staatsarchiv Marburg, Fiche No. Z.51158.

Marrion, Robert J. "2nd (Bayreuth) Regiment of Ansbach-Bayreuth, 1777-83" *Military Historian and Collector* no. 52 (Fall 2000): 136-137.

Mayer, Lloyd M. "The Dedication of Butts Hill Fort." *Bulletin of the Newport Historical Society*. no. 47 (November 1923).

Meyer, Bernd. "St. Georgen Monument to von Seyboth." *Nordbayerischer Kurier Bayreuth (Heimatkurier)* no. 3 (1997).

Monatlischer Rapport, Regiment von Bünau, September 1778. Library of Congress from Preussiches Staatsarchiv Marburg.

Pawtucket Archaeological Laboratories, *PAL Report #950: Archaeological Survey, Pawtucket, Rhode Island*. Pawtucket, Rhode Island: Pawtucket Archaeological Laboratories, 1998.

———. *PAL Report # 963: Archaeological Investigation: Great Friends Meeting House, Newport*. Pawtucket, Rhode Island: Pawtucket Archaeological Laboratories, 1999.

Peebles, John. *John Peeble's American War: The Diary of a Scottish Grenadier, 1776–1782*, edited by Ira D. Gruber. Stroud, Gloucestershire: Sutton, for the Army Records Society, 1997.

Pettengill, Ray Waldron. *Letters from America 1776-1779: Being Letters of Brunswick, Hessian, and Waldeck Officers with the British Armies during the Revolution*. Boston: Houghton Mifflin, 1924.

A Plan of a Battery of Six Guns and Redoubt, Collection of John T. Pierce, Sr., Portsmouth, Rhode Island.

Popp, Stephan. *A Hessian Soldier in the American Revolution: The Diary of Stephan Popp*. Translated by Reinhart J. Pope, 1953.

———. *Popp's Journal, 1777-1783*. Translated by Joseph G. Rosengarten. Philadelphia: Historical Society of Pennsylvania, 1902.

Powel, H.W.H. "Early Defenses of Newport During Siege in 1778." *The Bulletin of the Newport Historical Society* 47 (November 1923): 23-24.

Prechtel, Johann Ernst. *A Hessian Officer's Diary of the American Revolution*. Translated by Bruce E. Burgoyne. Bowie, Maryland: Heritage Press, 1994.

Preston, Howard Willis. *The Battle of Rhode Island. August 29, 1778*. Providence: State Bureau of Information, 1928.

———. *Rhode Island's Historic Background*. Providence: Remington Press for the State Bureau of Information, 1930.

Pyle, Katherine. *Once Upon a Time in Rhode Island*. Garden City, New York: Doubleday, Page and Company in association with the Society of the Colonial Dames in Rhode Island, 1914.

"Reenact–200th Anniversary." *Phoenix Times*, August 30-31, 1978.

Rhode Island Historical Preservation Commission. *Historic and Architectural Resources of Jamestown, Rhode Island*. Providence: Rhode Island Historical Preservation Commission, 1995.

___. *Historic and Architectural Resources of Middleton, Rhode Island: A Preliminary Report.* Providence: Rhode Island Historical Preservation Commission, 1979.

___. *North Kingstown, Rhode Island, Statewide Historical Preservation Report W-NK-1.* Providence: Rhode Island Historical Preservation Commission, 1979.

___. *Historic and Architectural Resources of Portsmouth, Rhode Island: A Preliminary Report.* Providence: Rhode Island Historical Preservation Commission, 1979.

Rhode Island Historical Society. *What a Difference a Bay Makes.* Providence: Rhode Island Historical Society, 1993.

Rosengarten, Joseph G. "A Defense of the Hessians." *Pennsylvania Magazine of History* 23 (1899): 157-183.

___. "The German Soldiers in Newport 1776-1779 and the Siege of 1778." *The Rhode Island Historical Magazine* 7, no. 2 (October 1886).

Schwalm, Mark A. *The Hessians—Auxiliaries to the British Crown in the American Revolution (A Series of Four Lectures).* Grantham, Pennsylvania: Palatines to America, Pennsylvania Chapter, Messiah College, September 22, 1984.

Seidel, Jochen. "Juchhe nach Amerika!—Der Einsatz fränkischer Truppen im Amerikanischen Unabhängigkeitskrieg." http://www.jochen-seidel.de/kulma/usa1777.htm

Selig, Robert A. "A German Soldier in New England During the Revolutionary War: The Account of Georg David Flohr." *Newport History* no. 223, Part 2 (Fall 1993): 48–65.

Simister, Florence Parker. *The Fire's Center: Rhode Island in the Revolutionary Era, 1763-1790.* Providence: Rhode Island Bicentennial Foundation, 1979.

Stang, George Adam. "March Routes of George Adam Stang, Oboist, Bayreuth, 19 January 1784." Translated and annotated by Bruce E. Burgoyne, *Johannes Schwalm Historical Association* 5, no. 2 (1994). (Original German document in the Nürnberg State Archives in Germany)

Taylor, Erich A. O'D. *Campaign on Rhode Island MDCCLXXVIII.* Newport, 1928.

Terry, Roderick. "The Story of Green End Fort at the Siege of Newport." *The Bulletin of the Newport Historical Society* 51 (October 1924): 7–14.

Thalmann, G.F. *Fahnen und Uniformen der Landgräflich Hessen-Kassel'schen Truppen im Amerikanischen Unabhängigkeitskrieg 1776-1783.* Marburg: Hessisches Staatsarchiv Marburg, 1977.

Troiani, Don. *Soldiers in America: 1754-1865.* Mechanicsburg, Pennsylvania: Stackpole, 1998.

Waldenfels, Otto von. *Die Freiherrn von Waldenfels, II.* Teil. Munich: Pasing, 1959.

Wasmus, J.F. *An Eyewitness Account of the American Revolution and New England Life: The Journal of J. F. Wasmus, German Company Surgeon, 1776-1783.* Edited by Mary C. Lynn, translated by Helga Doblin. New York: Greenwood Press, 1990.

Wende, C. [Regimental Quartermaster (German)]. *Journal of Regiment Von Ditfurth, North American Campaign.* Marburg: Hessen-Kasselisches Archiv. Kriegssachen. O.W.S. 1268, CXXV, box 2416.

Wheeler, Robert L. "Bloody Battle of Rhode Island." *The Rhode Island Magazine.* (December 13, 1953).

Woodward, Carl R. *Plantation in Yankeeland: the Story of Cocumscussoc, Mirror of Colonial Rhode Island.* Chester, Connecticut: Pequot Press, 1971.

Index

Abbatis, 102, 103

Advocate, 87

Alexander, Margrave Christian Friedrich Carl, 8, 24-25, 33, 35, 38, 40, 52, 88, 125

Almy, Benjamin and Mary, 145

Congress, 14, 71, 144, 155, 157

American Revolution, 9, 11, 23, 171

Ambush, 144

Anabaptist, 69, 89

Anhalt-Zerbst, 19, 23, 33, 40

Ansbach, 8, 25, 38, 53, 129, 135, 145, 149-150, 154, 155, 162

Ansbach-Bayreuth, 8, 19, 21, 23-24, 33, 37-38, 52, 87-88, 93, 123, 125-127, 143, 145-146, 149, 153, 155, 157, 167, 169

Anthony Hill, 7, 102, 148, 150

Aquidneck Island, 3, 73, 172

Arnberg, Major von, 163-164

Army of Occupation, 100

Arnold's Point, 112

Articles of Association, 104

Articles of War, 35

Asteroth, Johann Valentin, 43, 50, 59, 98

Atlantic Ocean, 22, 30, 32, 40, 42, 54, 73, 75

Auditor, 34, 87

Austria, 9, 17

Auxiliary Troops, 25

Avant Guard (Chasseurs), 155

Azores, 42, 52, 53

Barton, Lt. Col. William, 73, 83, 85, 115

Baptist, 69, 89, 114

Barrington, Capt., 83

Barrington Hill, 102, 137, 146

Battle of Rhode Island, 143, 145, 147, 156, 167, 171, 177

Bayreuth, 39, 53, 94, 131, 138

Bayreuther Zeitungen, 80, 82, 112, 149-150, 155, 166

Beavertail, 17, 127, 175

Bedford (New Bedford), 107

Black Point, 122

Black Regiment, 173
Bliss Hill, 102
Block Island, 52
Blockage, 132
Blood Money, 23
Bloody Run Brook, 156
Bohemia, 89
Bonn, 88
Bordentown, 62
Bose, Col. C. von, 79, 105, 162
Boston, 1, 10, 11, 12, 14, 17, 76, 141, 156
Boston Massacre, 11
Boston Tea Party, 12
Bourbonnais, 176
Bowler, Judge Metcalf, 91
Brandenburg, House of, 125, 168
Bremerhaven, 37
Bremerlehe, 37, 42, 46, 88
Brenton's Point, 100, 128, 133, 140, 163-164
Brenton's Neck, 75, 122, 131, 137
Brigade, Hessian, 5
Bristol, 10, 17, 77, 80, 110, 112-113, 115, 122
Bristol Ferry, 115
British High Command, 58
Brown, Brig. Gen., 122
Brown's Corp of Provincials, 122, 129, 135, 150, 157, 163
Brunswick, 19, 23, 27, 37, 41
Burgoyne, Gen., 101, 120
Burrington Hill, 147
Butts Hill (Windmill Hill), 7, 75, 102, 104, 109, 117, 122, 135-136, 138, 145, 151, 157, 173, 176
Byron, Admiral, British, 139
Campbell, Lt. Col. John, 7, 63, 112-113, 122, 144
Canada, 120
Card's Redoubt, 102
Carnegie Abbey Golf Club, 156, 173
Catherine the Great, Empress, Russia, 15
Catholics, 89
Chaplain(s), 34, 87
Charleston, 10, 167
Chasseurs, 6, 31, 63, 75, 82, 98, 109, 112, 114-115, 122, 133, 136, 143-146, 150, 162, 167, 173
Church of England, 89
Churches, 69, 114
Clayton, Ships Capt., 112
Clinton, General Sir Henry, 1, 2, 6, 62, 77, 81, 91, 125, 153-154, 157, 172
Coaster's Harbor Island, 5
Coddington's Cove, 83, 99, 136
Colony House (Newport), 69, 174
Commissioners of Peace, 156
Common Fence Neck, 73, 80, 115, 118

INDEX

Conanicut Battery, 3, 175-176

Conanicut Island, 3, 7, 14, 17, 77, 82, 97-100, 109-111, 122, 127, 129-133, 136-137, 140, 142, 153, 157, 163

Concord, 14

Congregational Church, 69, 76, 148

Congress, 14, 71, 144, 155, 157

Continentals, 83, 100

Continental Navy, 14

Cornwallis, Gen., 61, 167

Cornell, Col. Ezekiel, 145

Court Martials, 92

Cutler, Rev. Manassah, 148

Dartmouth, Lord, 1, 14

Declaration of Independence, 18, 120

Delaware River, 61

Desertions, 71

d'Estaing, Admiral Hector, 120, 132, 135, 138-140, 142, 175

Destailleur, Doctor, Brit. Arty., 65

Diaries of Chaplain Heinrich Kümmel, 50

Diary of Johann Ernst Prechtel, 163

Discipline, 70, 91

Ditfurth, Lt. Gen. von, 81, 156, 162, 166

Döhla, Johann Conrad, 153

Dordrecht, 53

Double Allegiance, 26

Drummund, Sea Capt., 94

Dumplings Battery, 98, 100, 110, 127-129, 132-133, 157-158

Dutch Island, 98-99

Dyer's Island, 3

Easton's Beach, 109, 133, 157

Easton's Redoubt, 121

East Ferry, 14

East India Company, 12, 138

East River, 60

East (Main) Road, 143-145

Elam's Farm, 122, 156

Elbe River, 37

English Church, 89-90, 164, 175

Engs, Quaker family, 94

Episcopal Church, 114

Erb, Chaplain, 88, 157

Eyb, Col. Friedrich Ludwig Albrecht von, 125

Eyre, Maj., 115

Fall River, 115

Fanning, Col., 135, 146, 150, 163-164

Faucitt, Col. William, 17, 19, 33, 52

First Division, 42, 45

Flatbush, 60

flogging, 92

Fogland Ferry, 75, 100, 102, 109, 117, 122, 133

Foreigners for enlistment, 28, 35

Fort Adams, 173

Fort Barton, 73, 85
Fort Brown, 163
Fort Fanning, 102
Fort George, 65, 140
Fort Green, 163
Fort Greene, 99
Fort Lee, 61
Fort Liberty, 65
Fort Tiverton Heights, 85
Fort Washington (New York), 60, 61, 62
Fox Hill, 127-129, 131-132
France, 9, 120
Franconians, 24, 87, 93, 125-127, 167, 173
Franken, 125
Franklin, Benjamin, 120
Frederick the Great (Friedrich der Große), 9, 15, 25, 30, 39, 40, 88, 125
Freeborn's Creek, 136, 156
French Fleet, 100, 123, 127, 129-133, 137, 140, 143, 151, 157, 162, 175
French and Indian War, 9
Friedrich II, Landgrave of Hesse, 8, 9, 22, 23, 26, 27, 82
Gage, Gen., 14
Gambier, Adm., 162-164
Gauntlet, 71, 92, 93, 162
Gemmingen, Freiherr Carl von, 33
German(s), 15, 20, 21, 28, 70, 71, 149, 167

Germany, 17, 57, 81, 88, 110, 125, 153-154, 167
Glover, General John, 145
Goat Island, 65, 93, 128, 137, 140
Greene, Gen. Nathanael, 145
Greene, George Washington, 177
Green End, 99, 127, 133, 138, 173-174
Green End Fort, 102
Grey, Maj. Gen. Charles, 142, 153, 157, 166
Grim, David, 61
Halifax, 17, 49
Hancock, John, 11, 71
Hanover Electorate, 19, 37
Hartford, 177
Heister, Lt. Gen. Leopold Philip von, 42, 58, 60
Hesse-Hanau, 19, 23, 33
Hesse-Kassel, 8, 19, 23, 25, 27, 31, 32, 33, 37
Hessian's Hole, 156
Historic Buildings, 174-175
Holland, 37, 38, 150
Honeyman's Hil, 102, 138, 141
Hopkins, Brig. Gen. Esek, 17, 97-99
Howe, Admiral Lord Richard, 1, 17, 50, 76, 138, 140, 141
Howe, General Sir William, 1, 59, 98, 125
Howland's Ferry, 73, 83, 107, 109, 112, 118, 138

INDEX

Hudson River, 61, 126
Hussars, 40
Huyn, Colonel J.C. von, 2, 6, 50, 70, 79, 91, 117
Illness, 87-88, 161
India, 9
Irish's Redoubt, 143
Jaeger (Jäger), 6, 31, 33, 38, 39, 101, 126
Jamestown (RI), 175
Jeremia Kappas Diary, 45
Journal of Captain Friedrich von der Malsburg, 144
Journal of Garrison Regiment von Huyn, 50, 74, 79, 93, 117, 132, 165
Journal of Leib-Infantry Regiment von Wutgenau, 162-163
Journal of Regiment von Ditfurth, 1, 45, 83, 137, 158-159
Journal of Regimernt von Bünau, 93
Kickemuit, 107, 112-113
King George II of Britain, 19
King George III of Britain, 14, 18, 19, 20, 32, 33
King Louis XVI of France, 126
King's Battery, 137
King's Rangers, 148
Kleinschmidt, G., Quartermaster, 42, 82
Klingender, Capt., 81
Kosputh, Maj. Gen. von, 162

Knowles, Lt., 43
Knyphausen, Lt. Gen. Freyherr Willhelm von, 42, 45, 58, 61, 62, 80, 112, 168
Kümmel, Heinrich, Chaplain, 88
Lafayette, General, 142
Land Grants, 71, 94
Landgrave, 8, 19, 22, 23, 26, 27, 82, 154, 162
Lange, Lt. Col., 52
Laurens, Col. John, 144
Lawton's Valley, 7, 102
Layton Mills, 122
Lee, Gen., Charles, 84, 122
Lehigh Hill, 102
Lexington, 14, 97
Livingston, Col. Henry B., 144-145
Long Island, 7, 52, 107
Lopez's House, 109
Lossberg, Col./Gen. Friedrich W. von, 2, 62, 79, 81, 105, 115, 117-119, 121-122, 142-143, 148-149, 155, 162
Loyalists, 161
Luther, Martin, 89
MacKenzie, Lt. Frederick, 4, 7, 70, 73, 75, 93, 98, 102, 109, 112, 118, 122, 127, 129, 131-133, 136-138, 140-143, 146, 149-150, 153-154, 157-158
Mainz, 37
Main River, 37, 38

Malsburg, Capt. Friederich von der, 5, 7, 63, 64, 66, 70, 73, 75, 76, 89, 91, 100, 117, 122, 132-133, 135, 137, 141, 143-144, 146-148, 155-156, 162, 166

Marburg. 29

Margrave Carl Alexander, 8, 24, 25, 33, 35, 38, 40, 52, 88, 125

Martha's Vineyard, 157

Matthews, Gen., 163

Mercenaries, 25, 26

Meisheimer, Lt., 115

Miantonomi Park, 7, 173

Middletown, 8, 73, 102

Militia, 14, 17, 80, 97, 99-100, 142

Minutemen, 108

Mobilization, 27

Molitor, Capt. Christian T.S., 94

Monthly Reports, 94

Moravian, 69

Motz, Sr. Auditor, 59

Mount Hope Bay, 115

Music, 65

Mutiny, 38, 52

Narragansett, 1, 3, 10, 12, 14, 17, 77, 85, 97, 99, 108, 127, 131-132, 140, 142, 153, 157, 163-164, 175

Navigation Acts, 10

New Beford (Bedford), 107, 157

New Foundland, 42, 49

New London, 163

Newport, 1, 4, 5, 6, 7, 10, 11, 14, 17, 62, 63, 73, 76, 80, 81, 82, 83, 88, 91, 94, 97-102, 104, 109, 112, 117-118, 120-123, 129, 131, 135, 138, 141-143, 153, 157, 161, 164, 167, 172, 175

Newport Gazette, 89

New Rochelle, 52

Newton's Rangers, 108

New York, 1, 9, 10, 14, 17, 27, 33, 50, 52, 53, 59, 60, 70, 73, 85, 88, 94, 110, 112, 119, 125, 138, 142, 161, 167

Nijmegen, 52

Noltenius, Capt. August, 7, 112, 115, 117, 122, 144, 155, 162

North Kingstown, 108

North Battery, 128, 131, 137, 173

North Point, 99-100

North Sea, 37, 88

Nova Scotia, 94

Ochsenfurt, 38, 40, 52

Order of Battle, 145

Overing, Quaker, 8, 83

Palmer Brigade, 101

Papasquash Point, 113

Parker, Admiral Sir Peter, 2, 3

Parliament, 10

Pattison, Gen., 162

Pennsylvania, 94

Percy, Gen. Lord Hugh, 2, 6, 65, 75, 76, 81

INDEX

Philadelphia, 94, 126, 177

Pigot, Maj.Gen. Robert, 85, 91, 99, 101, 110, 122, 133, 143, 150-151, 154-155, 157

Point Bridge, 70

Point Judith, 108

Poplar Point, 108

Popp, Stephen, 145

Portsmouth, England, 42, 46, 53

Portsmouth, Rhode Island, 8, 75, 83, 91, 101, 149, 156, 172-173

Potsdam, 30

Potter House, 137

Prechtel, Lt. Johannes, 91, 92, 93, 129-130, 163-164

Presbyterian Church, 69, 75, 88

Prescott, Gen. Richard, 2, 7, 8, 63, 75, 81, 83, 84, 89, 122, 142-143, 151, 157, 164, 166

President John Hancock, 11, 71

Prince(s), 155

Prince of Wales American Volunteers, 122

Prison Ship, 133

Protestants, 89

Providence, 10, 14, 73, 75, 77, 84, 97, 107, 109, 120, 177

Providence Gazette, 155

Provincial Regiment, 122, 145

Provost, 87

Prudence Island, 15, 17, 73, 108, 136

Prussia, 9, 17, 23, 29, 30, 35, 40, 88, 125

Punishment, 93

Puritan, 69, 76

Quaker, 69, 70, 83, 89, 101, 154

Quaker Hill, 7, 102, 109, 122, 143, 145-146, 148

Quaker Meeting House, 88, 157

Quartering Act, 12

Quartermaster, 34, 79, 87

Quebec, 27, 33

Raids, 14-15, 107-108, 112, 115, 157

Rall, Col. von, 61, 62, 80

Rawdon, Lord, 65

Recruitment, 27, 157

Redwood Library, 68, 174

Regiments

British:

22nd, 63, 109, 112, 122, 135, 142-146, 149, 155

26th Light Infantry, 6, 31, 162

29th, 11

38th,123, 136, 143

43rd, 109, 122, 135, 143, 145, 150, 163

54th, 7, 82, 97, 109, 112, 122, 131, 136, 143, 149, 157, 163

63rd, 82

Corps of Light Horse, 1

Hessian:
  DuCorps (Leib), 1, 5, 32, 79, 82, 105
  Landgrave (Wutgenau), 1, 5, 7, 33,79, 80, 82, 101, 105, 109, 121-122, 135, 148, 150, 162-163, 167
  Prinz Karl (Prinz Carl), 1, 5, 32, 79, 82
  von Bünau, 1, 5, 7, 33, 79, 82, 87, 94, 98, 109, 117-118, 121-122, 136, 162
  von Ditfurth, 1, 5, 7, 32, 46, 63, 79-80, 81, 82, 87, 109, 117, 121-122, 135-136, 148, 150, 155, 167
  von Huyn, 1, 5, 7, 33, 79, 82, 87, 98, 109, 117, 121-122, 135, 145-146, 148, 150, 155, 163-164, 166-167

Replacements, 157

Revolutionary War, 32, 120, 173

Rhode Island, 1, 3, 17, 49, 62, 73, 76, 82, 94, 100, 105,107, 109-110, 112, 117-118, 125, 135, 142, 145, 151, 161, 172

Rhineland, 176

Rhine River, 37, 38, 88

Riedesel, Gen. von, 55

Ritzebüttel, 42

Rochambeau, Comte de, 176-177

Roepanack, Lt., 122

Rose Island, 100

Rosengarten, J.G., 177

Royal Artillery, 122-123

Royal Deux-Ponts, 176

Russia, 9

St. John's Day, 70

Saintonge, 176

Sandy Hook, 42, 49, 120

Sakonnet River, 97, 135, 173

Saratoga, 27, 101, 120

Saxony, 9

Schleenstein, Capt., 122

Schmeer, Corp. Conrad, 52

Schmitt, Maj. Gen. Konrad, 2

Schöpp, Dr. Surgeon, 161

Second Division, 42, 50

Seir, Capt., 113

Seume, Johann Gottfried, 53

Seven Years' War, 9, 17, 54, 120

Seybothen, Col. Franz Johann Heinrich Wilhelm von, 35, 148

Sheffield, Elay, 5

Shelter Island, 74, 107-108

Ships
  Adamant, 52
  Cerberus, 136
  Cimetar, 100
  Cygnet, Man-of-War, 49
  Diamond, H.M.S., Frigate, 80
  Diana, Sloop, 14
  Five Sisters, 50
  Flora, 113
  Four Good Friends, 50

INDEX

Gaspee, 11
Juno, 100, 136
Katy, Sloop, 14
Lark, 136
Liberty, Sloop, 11
Maidstone, 12
Malaga, 48
Mermaid, 50
Orpheus, 136
Pigot Galley, 136
Raisonnable, 162
Renown, 108, 162
Rose, H.M.S., 12, 14
Scarborough, 100
Spring, 48
Squirrel, 12
St. John, 12
Talion, Frigate, 162
Tryals, 65
Unicorn, 83
Siege, 139, 141, 157
Slaves, Slave Trade, 10
Smallpox, 87
Smith, Brig. Gen., 142-143
Soissonnais, 176
Social Events, 65, 68
Sons of Liberty, 11
South Kingstown, 108, 163
Spain, 9
Spencer, Gen., 100-101
Staff Functions, 87
Stamp Act, 10

Staten Island, 50, 52, 53, 57, 59, 125
Stoddard House, 137
Subsidy Agreement, 19, 25, 26, 27, 28
Suffolk, Lord, 17
Sugar Act, 10
Sullivan, Maj. Gen. John, 100, 120, 135, 138-139, 141-146, 148, 150, 153, 155-156, 172, 173, 175
Surgeon, 34, 87
Synagogue, 69, 89, 174
Taxes, 10
Thames Street (Newport), 68, 70
Thomas, Soldier Christian, 98
Tiverton, 77, 83, 85, 97, 110, 135, 138, 176
Tonomy Hill, 5, 7, 99, 118, 131, 133, 135, 138, 173
Tory, Tories, 67, 93, 164
Toulon, 120
Town House and Court, 69
Townshend, Lord Charles, 10, 11
Treaty of Alliance, 120
Treaty of Paris, 120
Trenton, 61, 80, 82
Trinity Church (Newport), 89, 90, 164, 175
Trinity Church (New York), 60
Trumbull, Col. John, 148
Trümbach, Regt. von, 32, 162

Tyler, Brig. Gen. John, 145
Turkey Hill, 7, 102, 122, 146, 148, 150
Union Street, 144
United States of America, 171
Varnum, Gen. James Mitchell, 145
Vergennes, Count, 120
Virginia, 120, 167
Voit von Salzburg, Col. Friedrich August Valentine, 35, 127, 162
Vultejus, Capt. George, 94
Waldeck, 19, 23, 27, 37, 42, 52
Wallace, Capt. James, 12, 14, 15, 17, 108
Wallenberger, Brigade Major, 65
War of Independence, 14, 25
Warren, 17, 108, 112-114, 122
Warren River, 113-114
Warwick, 11, 80, 83
Washington, Gen. George, 60, 61, 80, 120, 135, 177
Weaver's Cove, 3
Wende, Quartermaster Christoph, 1, 79, 82, 87
Weser River, 37, 40
West (Main)Road, 83, 102, 122, 143, 145-146, 148, 150, 173
West Passage, 3, 131, 162, 175
West Point, 177
Wheeler, Robert, 172

Whitehall (Berkely House), 6
White Plains, 62
Wickford, 108
Wien, Commissary Gen., 163
Windmill Hill (Butts Hill), 7, 75, 80, 102-103, 109, 117, 122, 135-136, 138, 145, 151, 157, 173, 176
Yorktown, 167, 171, 177
Zerbst, 19, 23, 33, 40
Zweibrücken, 176

About the Author

Walter Schroder was born in Rhode Island, the son of German immigrants. A resident of Jamestown for thirty-two years, he now lives in North Kingstown with his wife Lora.

He spent the years of his youth in Germany, where he attended school and was drafted to serve with an antiaircraft battery at age fifteen near the end of WW-II. As a prisoner of war he functioned as an interpreter until discharged in West Germany in 1946. He enlisted in the U.S. Army of Occupation in 1948 and received his basic training at Marburg, Germany, after which he was assigned to duties that enabled him to fully employ his language skills.

Following his discharge in America, he completed a civilian career with the Defense Department, retiring in 1989 after thirty-one years of service. At that time he was awarded the Navy's Superior Civilian Service Medal. He was subsequently employed as Training Officer for the Rhode Island Emergency Management Agency for four years.

He has a special interest in Rhode Island's military history and has authored five books in that field, including *Defenses of Narragansett Bay in World War II*, now in its ninth printing. His autobiography *Stars and Swastikas: The Boy Who Wore Two Uniforms*, has been the focus of various school projects. He has lectured extensively and has appeared on NBC10 *Timelines* and Public Television.

In researching *The Hessian Occupation of Newport and Rhode Island, 1776–1779*, he has found his firsthand knowledge of German script and military terminology to be very helpful.

www.ingramcontent.com/pod-product-compliance
Lightning Source LLC
Chambersburg PA
CBHW051922160426
43198CB00012B/2000